Henry D Wireman

Gems of German lyrics

Consisting of selections from Rueckert, Lenau, Chamisso, Freiligrath and others

Henry D Wireman

Gems of German lyrics
Consisting of selections from Rueckert, Lenau, Chamisso, Freiligrath and others

ISBN/EAN: 9783742891341

Hergestellt in Europa, USA, Kanada, Australien, Japan

Cover: Foto ©Thomas Meinert / pixelio.de

Manufactured and distributed by brebook publishing software
(www.brebook.com)

Henry D Wireman

Gems of German lyrics

GEMS

OF

GERMAN LYRICS:

CONSISTING OF

SELECTIONS FROM RUECKERT, LENAU,
CHAMISSO, FREILIGRATH
AND OTHERS.

BY

HENRY D. WIREMAN.

PHILADELPHIA:
CLAXTON, REMSEN & HAFFELFINGER,
1869.

MEICHEL & PLUMLY, Printers, Third and Race.

TO

MY MOTHER.

PREFACE.

An ardent admirer of Poetry, it was not until I became familiar with the authors of "Refuge," "The Dying Flower," "The Echo," "The Dead Soldier" and some others, that I fully realized the *beauties* of the Lyric Muse. For truth to Nature, pathos and simplicity of style, appealing as they do to the finest feelings of the human heart, there are, in my estimation, no sweeter poems than Lenau's "Refuge" and "Gaze Into The Stream."

The more deeply I entered into this sacred realm of thought, the more deeply it impressed me, and the greater became my enthusiasm, until at length I found myself worshiping at its shrine. Many were the poems that greeted me, some so congenial to my day dreams and fancies, that I could not resist the

temptation of rendering them into English; select-
ing them for the sentiments embodied, the musical
purity of the versification, or for their applicability
to some incident in the history of my life; not then
with a view to publication, but merely for my own
amusement and gratification

Many of these poems are therefore dear friends.
I need but recur to them, to have the memories of
the past, with which they are inseparably connected,
rise vividly before me; even like the repetition of
a melody, once heard allied with some incident of
moment in our lives, all the associations connected
with its first rendition are revived, and we revel in
the memories thereof.

Who, that has wandered alone in a foreign land,
where the scenes, the people and their customs
were new, and even the human voice itself was
dead, has not, when hearing a melody he often
heard his mother sing, thought of her, and longed to
be at home again, if but for a moment, to peep in
at the " Home Circle," to see what the loved ones

might be doing? Cannot he better appreciate Cha-
misso's "Homesickness" and Siebel's "Home," than
one who has never wandered from the shelter of his
father's roof?

Finding however that I had gradually accumulated
quite a number of translations, and seeing so large a
field open for a book of this kind, I concluded,
though with great diffidence, from my youth and in-
experience, to submit my humble effort to the public.
I have been careful to include only those Poets who
were but little known to persons on this side of the
Atlantic, unacquainted with the German; those that
have not been, as far as I have been able to ascer-
tain, with but few exceptions, already translated.
Having strayed from the beaten path, and gathered
flowers where few are wont to ramble, the lyrics of
those master minds, SCHILLER and GOETHE, and of
favorites like HEINE and GEIBEL, have been omitted.

If my interpretations, have rendered these authors
in a clear and intelligible form, presenting the pic-
ture as the Author painted it, still retaining a pure

versification, I am well satisfied; and I may use with slight variation, the words of Coleridge:

"I expect neither profit nor fame from my writings; and I consider myself amply repaid without either. The study of the German Poets has been to me 'its own exceeding great reward'; it has soothed my afflictions; it has multiplied and refined my enjoyments; it has endeared solitude; and it has given me the habit of wishing to discover the Good and the Beautiful in all that meets and surrounds me."

THE AUTHOR.

PHILADELPHIA, JUNE, 1869.

Inhalt.

CONTENTS.

PAGE.

Gems of German Lyrics.

Zuflucht.

Armes Wild im Waldesgrunde,
Schlägt die Jagd dir eine Wunde,
Flüchtest du zur tiefsten Stelle,
An des Walds geheimste Quelle,
Daß sie dir mit frischer Kühle
Lindernd deine Wunde spüle.

Mensch, du flieh mit deinem Schmerz
An die heimathlichste Stelle,
An des Trostes reinste Quelle,
Flüchte an das Mutterherz.
Doch die Mütter sterben bald;
Hat man dir begraben deine,
Flüchte in den tiefsten Wald
Mit dem wunden Reh—und weine!

Lenau.

REFUGE.

ARMLESS deer in forest ground,
    When thou dost receive a wound,
Flec'st thou to the deepest nook,
To the wood's most secret brook;
That the waters cool and fresh
Soothe thy torn and quiv'ring flesh.

Man, if thou afflicted be,
To the home-like, dearest nook,
Consolation's clearest brook,
To the mother heart Oh, flee!
Mothers all, alas! must die;
Oh, if thine hath gone to sleep,
To the deepest forest fly
With the wounded deer, and weep!

LENAU.

O süße Mutter!

süße Mutter,
Ich kann nicht spinnen,
Ich kann nicht sitzen
Im Stübchen innen,
Im engen Haus;
Es stockt das Rädchen,
Es reißt das Fädchen,
O süße Mutter,
Ich muß hinaus.

„Der Frühling gucket
Hell durch die Scheiben;
Wer kann nun sitzen,
Wer kann nun bleiben
Und fleißig sein?
O laß mich gehen,
Und laß mich sehen,
Ob ich kann fliegen
Wie Vögelein.

OH, MOTHER DEAR!

II, mother dear,
    I cannot spin,
I cannot sit
This room within,
My narrow home;
The wheel doth quake,
The thread doth break,
Oh, mother dear,
Do let me roam !

"Spring brightly looks
Through yonder pane;
Who now can sit,
Who can remain
And busy be ?
Oh, let me go,
Run to and fro,
Then will I bring
A smile for thee !

„O laß mich sehen,
O laß mich lauschen,
Wo Lüftlein wehen,
Wo Bächlein rauschen,
Wo Blümlein blühn.
Laß sie mich pflücken,
Und schön mir schmücken
Die braunen Locken
Mit buntem Grün.

„Und kommen Knaben
In wilden Haufen,
So will ich traben,
So will ich laufen,
Nicht stille stehn;
Will hinter Hecken
Mich hier verstecken,
Bis sie mit Lärmen
Vorüber gehn.

"Oh, let me fly,
Oh, let me go
Where zephyrs sigh,
Where streamlets flow
Thro' fragrant bow'rs.
Let me entwine
The em'rald vine,
And wreathe my brow
With fairest flow'rs.

"If boys approach
In boist'rous glee,
Then will I run,
Then will I flee,
I will not stay;
Will quickly hide,
And then abide,
Till they with shouts
Have passed away!

„Bringt aber Blumen
Ein frommer Knabe,
Die ich zum Kranze
Just nöthig habe:
Was soll ich thun?
Darf ich wohl nickend,
Ihm freundlich blickend,
O süße Mutter,
Zur Seit' ihm ruhn?"

Friedrich Rückert.

"But should a youth
Bring choicest spray,
Which I just need
For garland gay;
Oh, wilt thou chide,
If with sweet smile,
A little while,
I, mother dear,
Rest by his side?"

FRIEDRICH RUECKERT.

Das Mädchen und der Schmetterling.

Lustwandelnd schritt ein Mädchen
   In kühlem Waldesgrund,
Und als sie dort sich bückte,
Zum Strauß sich Blumen pflückte,
Da kam ein bunter Falter
Und küßte ihren Mund.

„Verzeih' mir," sprach der Falter,
„Verzeih' mir mein Vergehn,
Ich wollte Honig nippen
Und hatte deine Lippen,
Dein rothes, rothes Mündchen,
Für Rosen angesehn."

THE MAIDEN AND THE BUTTERFLY.

So gaily thro' the woods
    A sprightly maiden trips,
And as she stoops to pick,
For a nosegay, flowers quick,
A passing butterfly
Doth kiss her rosy lips.

The butterfly exclaims:
"Forgive me, maiden fair,
I honey wished to sip;
And Oh, I thought that lip,
That ruddy lip of thine,
A rose a blooming there!"

Da sprach zu ihm das Mädchen:

„Für diesmal, kleines Ding,

Will ich dir gern vergeben;

Doch merke dir daneben:

Nicht blühen diese Rosen

Für jeden Schmetterling.“

R. C. Wegener.

"This once, thou little thing,"

Thus doth the maid reply—

"Thou art forgiven; though

I fain would have thee know,

These roses do not bloom

For every butterfly!"

R. E. WEGENER.

Der todte Soldat.

Auf ferner fremder Aue
    Da liegt ein todter Soldat,
Ein ungezählter, vergeff'ner,
Wie brav er gekämpft auch hat.

Es reiten viel Generale
Mit Kreuzen an ihm vorbei;
Denkt keiner, daß, der da lieget,
Auch werth eines Kreuzleins sei.

Es ist um manchen Gefall'nen
Viel Frag' und Jammer dort,
Doch für den armen Soldaten
Gibt's weder Thräne noch Wort.

THE DEAD SOLDIER.

N a distant field a soldier
   Lies bleeding where he fell,
Unseen and ay, forgotten,
Although he fought so well.

Gen'rals bedecked with honors
Ride by where he doth rest;
None think of *his* deserving
To wear them on his breast.

For many of the fallen,
Here bitter tears are shed,
But of this poor, dead soldier,
E'en not a word is said.

Doch ferne, wo er zu Hause,

Da sitzt, beim Abendroth,

Ein Vater voll banger Ahnung

Und sagt: „Gewiß, er ist todt!"

Da sitzt eine weinende Mutter,

Und schluchzet laut: „Gott helf'!

Er hat sich angemeldet:

Die Uhr blieb stehn um Elf!"

Da starrt ein blasses Mädchen

Hinaus in's Dämmerlicht:

„Und ist er dahin und gestorben,

Meinem Herzen stirbt er nicht!"

At home a father sitteth,

West glows the evening red,

And, filled with strange forebodings,

Exclaims: "My boy is dead!"

There sits a mother weeping,

Who moans: " Help, Thou in Heav'n

I saw his apparition,——

The clock stopped at elev'n!"

A maiden pale, at twilight,

From reverie doth start:

"Though far away. and dying,

He lives within my heart!"

Drei Augenpaare schicken,

So heiß ein Herz nur kann,

Für den armen todten Soldaten

Ihre Thränen zum Himmel hinan.

Und der Himmel nimmt die Thränen

In einem Wölkchen auf,

Und trägt es zur fernen Aue

Hinüber im raschen Lauf;

Und gießt aus der Wolke die Thräne

Auf's Haupt des Todten als Thau,

Daß er unbeweint nicht liege

Auf ferner fremder Au'.

J. G. Seidl.

Three pairs of eyes now offer,

With warmth of hearts that love,

For one who fought so bravely,

Their tears, to Heaven above.

And Heaven these tears doth gather

Up in a cloud, which flies

To where the poor, dead soldier

On the field of battle lies.

As dew, these tears it poureth

Upon his brow, that lie

He might unwept for, never,

Where he, unknown did die.

J. G. SEIDL.

Maienthau.

Auf den Wald und auf die Wiese,
　Mit dem ersten Morgengrau,
Träuft ein Quell vom Paradiese,
Leiser, frischer Maienthau;
Was den Mai zum Heiligthume
Jeder süßen Wonne schafft,
Schmelz der Blätter, Glanz der Blume,
Würz' und Duft, ist seine Kraft.

Wenn den Thau die Muschel trinket,
Wird in ihr ein Perlenstrauß;
Wenn er in den Eichbaum sinket,
Werden Honigbienen d'raus;
Wenn der Vogel auf dem Reise
Kaum damit den Schnabel netzt,
Lernet er die helle Weise,
Die den ernsten Wald ergötzt.

MAY-DEW.

ON the mead and mossy mountain,
    At the peep of morning gray,
Drips from Paradise a fountain,
Soft and fresh, the dew of May;
That which May, a sacred power,
Gives to every heart's delight:
Leaves' enamel, glow of flower,
Sweetest fragrance, is its might.

When a shell its droplets drinketh,
Grows therein a pearl bouquet;
When it in the oak tree sinketh,
Honey-bees see light of day;
When the birdling scarcely wetteth
With it on the branch its bill,
It that wondrous song begetteth,
Which the wood with joy doth fill.

Mit dem Thau der Maienglocken

Wäscht die Jungfrau ihr Gesicht,

Badet sie die gold'nen Locken

Und sie glänzt von Himmelslicht;

Selbst ein Auge, roth geweinet,

Labt sich mit den Tropfen gern,

Bis ihm freundlich niederscheinet,

Thaugetränkt, der Morgenstern.

Sink' denn auch auf mich hernieder,

Balsam du für jeden Schmerz!

Netz' auch mir die Augenlider,

Tränke mir mein dürstend Herz!

Gib mir Jugend, Sangeswonne,

Himmlischer Gebilde Schau,

Stärke mir den Blick zur Sonne,

Leiser, frischer Morgenthau!

Ludwig Uhland.

Lilies fair the maid caresses,
Laves her face in dew-drops bright,
When she bathes her golden tresses,
She doth glow from Heav'nly light.
Gladly bathes an eye that weepeth
In these drops, in Heaven born,
Till so friendly on it peepeth,
Dew-bedrenched, the star of morn.

Sink on me a mortal dreary,
Balsam thou for every smart!
Moisten thou my eyelids weary,
Quench, Oh thou my thirsting heart!
Give me youth and songs of pleasure,
Heav'nly pictures let me view!
Turn my gaze to Heaven's treasure,
Soft and fresh, Oh morning dew!

LUDWIG UHLAND.

Die echte Thräne.

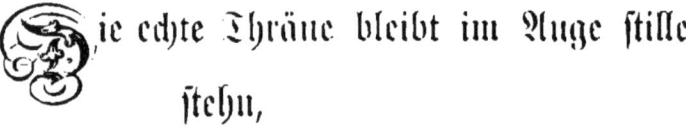

Die echte Thräne bleibt im Auge stille
stehn,

Sie fällt zur Erde nicht, kein Andres darf
sie sehn,

Kein Andres spricht von ihr in Mitleid nicht
noch Spott,

Daß sie geweinet ward, weiß Eines nur und
Gott.

Justinus Kerner.

THE REAL TEAR.

TILL in the eye remains the tear, that's
pure and real,

It falleth not to earth, doth not itself re-
veal,

No word of it in pity or in jest is said,

One only knows, and God, that it was

ever shed.

JUSTINUS KERNER.

Der Tod des Führers.

Von den Segeln tropft der Nebel,
Auf den Buchten zieht der Duft.
Zündet die Latern' am Maste!
Grau das Wasser, grau die Luft.
Todtenwetter!—zieht die Hüte!
Mit den Kindern kommt und Frau'n!
Betet! denn in der Kajüte
Sollt ihr einen Todten schau'n!"

Und die deutschen Ackersleute
Schreiten dem aus Boston nach,
Treten mit gesenktem Haupte
In das niedre Schiffsgemach:
Die nach einer neuen Heimath
Ferne steuern über's Meer,
Sehn im Todtenhemd den Alten,
Der sie führte bis hieher;

THE LEADER'S DEATH.

FROM the sails the fog is dripping,
   Mist is gath'ring on the bay,
At the mast go, light the lanterns!
Gray's the air, the water's gray.
Doff your hats!—of death the weather
Tells, bring women, children, shed
Tears and pray! for in the cabin
Lies one numbered with the dead!"

Deep in thought the German farmers
Pace the vessel's deck, and Oh!
Sadly weeping now, they enter
Still the little room below :
They who steer across the Ocean,
Seeking *new* homes far away,
See now in his grave-clothes lying,
Him who led them till this day;

Der aus leichten Tannenbrettern

Zimmerte den Hüttenkahn,

Der vom Neckar sie zum Rheine

Trug, vom Rhein zum Ozean;

Der, ein Greis, sich schweren Herzens

Losriß vom ererbten Grund;

Der da sagte: ,,,Laßt uns ziehen!

Laßt uns schließen einen Bund!'"

Der da sprach: ,,,Brecht auf nach Abend!

Abendwärts glüht Morgenroth!

Dorten laßt uns Hütten bauen,

Wo die Freiheit hält das Loth!

Dort laßt unsern Schweiß uns säen,

Wo kein todtes Korn er liegt!

Dort laßt uns die Scholle wenden,

Wo die Garben holt, wer pflügt!

Him who built the hut-like vessel
From the slender boards of pine,
Bearing them to Rhine from Neckar,
To the Ocean from the Rhine.
Him, who gray with age, with throbbing
Heart renounced his fatherland;
Him who said : " Oh, let us wander,
Let us form a solemn band! "

Him who spoke: "Our course is westward,
There the morning red doth glow,
Let us build our huts, where Justice
Weighs alike for high and low!
Where no rotten seed it layeth,
There, Oh, there, let's sow our sweat!
There too let us plow the earth, where
He who *sows*, the *fruit* doth get!

Laſſet unſern Herd uns tragen
In die Wälder tief hinein!
Laſſet mich in den Savannen
Euren Patriarchen ſein!
Laßt uns leben, wie die Hirten
In dem alten Teſtament!
Unſres Weges Feuerſäule
Sei das Licht, das ewig brennt!

Dieſes Lichtes Schein vertrau' ich,
Seine Führung führt uns recht!
Selig in den Enkeln ſchau' ich
Ein erſtandenes Geſchlecht!
Sie—ach, dieſen Gliedern gönnte
Noch die Heimath wohl ein Grab!
Um der Kinder willen greif' ich
Hoffend noch zu Gurt und Stab.

Let our humble hearths us carry

In the forest deep and free,

Let me through the western prairies,

Patriarch and Leader be!

Like the shepherds in the Bible

Let us live, ay, do as they !

Let our fiery pillar be, the

Light that brightly burns for aye !

For I trust this light's reflection,

It will lead us to the place,

Where from out our childrens' children

May spring up a happy race !

For these aching limbs, my country

Would me surely grant a grave,

For the children's sake, I full of

Hope, the weary journey brave !

Auf darum, und folgt aus Gosen
Der Vorangegangnen Spur!—'"
Ach, er schauete, gleich Mose'n,
Kanaan von ferne nur.
Auf dem Meer ist er gestorben,
Er und seine Wünsche ruhn;
Der Erfüllung und der Täuschung
Ist er gleich enthoben nun!

Rathlos die verlass'ne Schaar jetzt,
Die den Greis bestatten will.
Scheu verbergen sich die Kinder,
Ihre Mütter weinen still.
Und die Männer schaun beklommen
Nach den fernen Uferhöhn,
Wo sie fürder diesen Frommen
Nicht mehr bei sich wandeln sehn.

Up then, up! from Goshen follow,

Follow friends the guiding star!—"

But alas! he saw, like Moses,

Canaan only from afar.

On the Ocean he expired,

All his hopes and wishes rest;

From success and disappointment

Free alike now, he is blest.

Helpless now are they, who give the

Vet'ran's body to the deep,

Struck with awe, the children tremble,

And the mothers sadly weep.

And the men, too. gaze disheartened

At the friendless, distant shore,

Where they'll see their aged Leader

Them directing, nevermore.

„Von den Segeln tropft der Nebel,
Auf den Buchten zieht der Duft!
Betet! laßt die Seile fahren!
Gebt ihn seiner nassen Gruft!"
Thränen fließen, Wellen rauschen
Grellen Schrei's die Möve fliegt;
In der See ruht, der die Erde
Fünfzig Jahre lang gepflügt.

Ferdinand Freiligrath.

" From the sails the fog is dripping,

Mist is gath'ring on the bay !

Gently let the ropes go,—give him

To his watery grave—and pray!"

Shrieking harshly fly the seagulls,

Billows foam, fast flow the tears;

In the sea now resteth he, who

Plowed the earth for fifty years.

FERDINAND FREILIGRATH.

Sehnsucht.

Wenn durch die Lüfte wirbelnd treibt der
　　Schnee,

Und lauten Fußtritts durch die Flur der Frost

Einher geht auf der Spiegelbahn von Eis;

Dann ist es schön, geschützt vor Wintersturm

Und unvertrieben von der holden Gluth

Des eigenen Heerds, zu sitzen still daheim.

O dürft' ich sitzen jetzt bei Der daheim,

Die nicht zu neiden braucht den reinen Schnee,

Die mit der sonn'gen Augen sanfter Gluth

Selbst Funken weiß zu locken aus dem Frost!

Beschwören sollte sie in mir den Sturm,

Und thauen sollte meines Busens Eis.

LONGING.

WHEN through the air storm-beaten
whirls the snow,
And through the fields, with heavy foot-
steps, tramps
The frost upon the mirror path of ice:
How cozy then, well sheltered from the
storms
Of Winter, and never driven from the
hearth
Away, contented, still to sit at home.

Oh, could I only sit with *her* at home,
Who needs not envy e'en the purest snow,
Who with the sunny rays of her bright eyes,
Sparks even can entice from out the snow!
She should conjure in me the raging storm,
And thaw the ice concealed within my
breast.

Erst muß am Blick des Frühlinges das Eis

Des Winters schmelzen, und nach Norden heim,

Verscheucht vom Lenzhauch, ziehn der laute

    Sturm;

Eh' ich darf ziehn dorthin, wo ich den Schnee

Der Hand will küssen, den, weil Winterfrost

Ihn nicht erschuf, nicht tödtet Sommergluth.

Die Sehnsucht brennt in mir wie Sommer-

    gluth,

Aufzehrend innerlich, wie mürbes Eis,

Mein Herz, inmitten von des Winters Frost;

Und rastlos stäuben die Gedanken heim

Nach ihrem Ziel, sich kreuzend wie der Schnee,

Den flockend durcheinander treibt der Sturm.

Ay, at the glimpse of Spring, must melt
the ice
Of Winter first, and to its home far North,

Tempered by balmy airs, must flee the
storm,
Ere I can go, where I of that white hand

Could kiss the snow, which, since the
Winter's frost
Ne'er made it, Summer's heat can never
kill.

My longings burn in me like Summer's
heat,
Within consuming like decaying ice

My heart, amid the frost of Winter drear;

My restless thoughts do ever homeward
fly
Towards their goal, e'en like the drifted
snow,
When chased in all directions by the wind.

O daß mich faßend zu ihr trüg' ein Sturm,

Damit gestillet würde meine Gluth !

Und dürft' ich als ein Flöckchen auch von Schnee

Nur, oder als ein Nädelchen von Eis

Das Dach berühren, wo Sie ist daheim ;

Nicht fühlen wollt' ich da des Wintersfrost.

Wer fühlet, wo der Frühling athmet, Frost ?

Wen schrecket, wo die Liebe sonnet, Sturm ?

Wer kennet Ungemach, wo Sie daheim,

Sie, die mir zuhaucht sanfte Lebensgluth

So fern her, über manch Gefild von Eis

Und manch Gebirg, bedeckt von rauhem Schnee ?

Would but a storm catch me and take me
    off
To her, that stilled might be the fervor of

My heart! Oh, could I only touch as flake

The snow, or as a little crystal clear

Of ice, the roof where *she* doth sit at home!

I never more would feel the Winter's frost.

Who feels, where Spring doth breathe, the
    nipping frost?
Whom scares, where *love* doth dwell, the
    raging storm?
Who knoweth discomfort, where *she* is
    near?
She, who doth breathe to me the breath
    of *life*,
From distance far, o'er many a field of ice,

And many a rugged mount bedecked with
    snow.

Mit Blüthenschnee schmückt sich der kahle Frost,

Das Eis wird Lichtkristall und Wohllaut Sturm,

Wo ich voll Gluth zu Dir mich denke heim.

Friedrich Rückert.

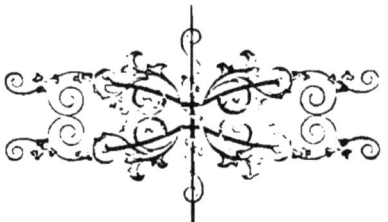

With snowy blossoms even the hoary frost

Attires itself, the ice to crystal turns,

The storm is lulled to sweetest sounds, when full

Of love I think myself with *thee* at home.

FRIEDRICH RUECKERT.

Das Echo.

Es irrt ein Mägdlein ganz allein
Auf ödem Pfade durch den Hain.

Es klagt und weint die Aenglein roth:

Seine Mutter, sagen sie, ist todt.

Und jammernd ruft es durch den Wald,

Daß laut das Echo wiederhallt:

„Wo bist du, Mutter? sage mir!"

Und horch! das Echo tönet: hier!

Das Mägdlein lauscht, ihm wird so bang',

Weiß nicht, woher die Stimme klang;

Schaut in das Thal, schaut in die Höh',

Fährt auf, wie ein gescheuchtes Reh,

Und läuft durch Dorn und Busch und Grund,

Das Kleid zerreißt, der Fuß ist wund:

THE ECHO.

 MAIDEN all alone doth roam,

On a rugged path afar from home,

She weeps e'en till her eyes grow red.

Alas! they say her mother is dead.

Thus through the woods she sadly cries,

And the echo to the sound replies:

" Where art thou? tell me, mother dear!"

And hark! the echo answers—" here!"

The maid doth list, knows not wherefrom

The voice, that gives her fear doth come;

She looks above, she looks below,

And, starting like a frightened doe,

She runs through thicket, bush and thorn;

Her feet are sore, her dress is torn.

Sie aber jammert durch den Wald,

Daß laut das Echo wiederhallt:

„Wo bist du, Mutter? sage mir!"

Und wieder tönt das Echo: hier!

Sie kam an eines Sees Rand,

Geschmückt mit Blumen allerhand,

Mit Rosen und mit Rosmarin,

Mit Trauerweiden dicht und grün.

Dem Kinde däucht die Fluth so blau,

Als ob's in's Mutterauge schau';

Die Welle rauscht so sanft, so weich,

Dem Wiegenlied der Mutter gleich:

„Wo bist du, Mutter? sage mir!"

Und aus den Wassern tönt es: hier!

Still through the woods she sadly cries,

And the echo to the sound replies :

" Where art thou ? tell me, mother dear ! "

Again the echo answers—"here ! "

She came to banks of lake so blue,

Bedecked with flowers of every hue;

The rose and lily here are seen,

And weeping willows thick and green.

So blue the stream, she thought, amazed,

Into her mother's eyes she gazed;

The wavelets ripple soft along,

E'en like her mother's cradle song:

" Where art thou? tell me, mother dear ! "

From out the depths a voice cries—"here!"

Da schwillt vor Ungeduld ihr Herz,

Und heitern Auges, ohne Schmerz,

Rasch in die Fluth stürzt sie hinein:

„Nun hab' ich dich, lieb Mütterlein!"

Robert Eduard Prutz

Impatience swells her throbbing heart,

She feels no more affliction's smart;

But leaps into the lake so clear:

"I HAVE THEE NOW, OH, MOTHER DEAR!"

ROBERT EDUARD PRUTZ.

Die Alpenrose.

Hoch auf dem Berg, im braunen Moose,
Von Eis umglänzt und halb verschneit,
Blüht still empor die Alpenrose:
Ein süß Gedicht der Einsamkeit.

Der lauen Frühlingslüfte Fächeln
Küßt ihre jungen Blätter nicht;
Sie steht wie ein verloren Lächeln
Im starren Felsenangesicht.

Die kalten Gletscherwände steigen
Anthürmend mächtig Stück für Stück,
Und unbemerkt im ew'gen Schweigen
Wächst sie wie ein verschwiegen Glück.

THE ALPINE-ROSE.

On moss, on mountain high, doth glow
  The Alpine-Rose, in its retreat
Of ice, well nigh concealed by snow :
Of solitude a poem sweet.

Spring's balmy zephyrs, mid the frost,
Ne'er kiss its leaves; in awful space
It blooms, e'en like a joy that's lost,
Upon the mountain's rugged face.

The glaciers stern, 'mong blast and chill,
Majestic, grand to Heaven loom,
Unnoticed in eternal still,
It like some silent joy doth bloom.

O selig der, dem wohlgeborgen,

Im oft durchfrosteten Gemüth,

Hoch über allen Erdensorgen

So eine süße Blume blüht!

Feodor Löwe.

Thrice happy he, in whom there glows,

Concealed in heart, deep frosted oft,

High over all the earthly woes,

Just such a flow'ret, pure and soft.

FEODOR LOEWE.

Gewisse Worte.

Worte gibt's, die nie verhallen,

Sie sind wie Steinchen, die gefallen

In einen Brunnen schwarz und tief,

Und die von Kant' zu Kante springen

Und stets von neuem aufwärts klingen,

Wenn scheinbar längst ihr Ton entschlief.

Es sind die Worte, die sich senken

In unsers Herzens tiefen Schacht:

Aus der Vergessenheiten Nacht

Klingt ewig neu ihr Angedenken.

CERTAIN WORDS.

THER'RE certain words that ring for aye,

    Like stones, dropt from our hands,

    are they,

Into a well so dark and deep,

And which from side to side do bound,

Sending upward anew the sound,

That one had thought long gone to sleep.

They are the words that sink into

Our heart's most secret, deep recess :

Out of the dark forgetfulness

The thought of them rings ever new.

Ich kehrte heim nach langen Jahren;

Des Lebens Wucht hatt' ich erfahren,

Gekostet auch des Lebens Freude:

Mit meiner Jugend zahlt' ich beide.

Die Mutter hielt mich lang umfangen,

Und als die erste Lust gestillt,

Sprach sie mit Tönen, traurig=mild:

O Gott, wie blaß sind deine Wangen!

O Gott, wie blaß sind deine Wangen!

Es glückt mir nicht, aus meinem Herzen

Die Mutterworte auszumerzen,

Ob Jahre d'rüber hingegangen.

Years had elapsed—home I returned,

Life's weight, how heavy, I had learned,

Had tasted all its sweets—forsooth

The price was high, it cost me youth.

My mother pressed me to her heart,

As if she feared again to part,

Then spoke in tones caressing, mild :

"Oh God, how pale thy cheeks, my child!"

"Oh God, how pale thy cheeks, my child!"

My mother's words will from my heart

Ay, never, nevermore depart,—

Those words so sad and yet so mild.

Ob nun in Freude, ob in Leide,

Der Wangen Frühling von mir scheide:

Die Worte sind mein treu Geleite.

Ich höre stets an meiner Seite

In Tönen traurigen und bangen:

O Gott, wie blaß sind deine Wangen!

Und sitz' ich Nachts allein und schaue

Mit falt'ger Stirne, düstrer Braue

Tief zu des Bechers gold'nem Grunde,

Ist mir, als ob aus treuem Munde

Heraus die Klageworte klangen:

O Gott, wie blaß sind deine Wangen!

If from my cheeks do now in gladness

The roses fade, or if in sadness,

These words remain my faithful guide.

I'm ever hearing at my side

In tones so mournful, quiet, mild :

"Oh God, how pale thy cheeks, my child !"

Gaze in the wine-glass I at night,

With ruffled brow and tear-dimmed sight,

When all is still and no one near,

Methinks from lips so true I hear,

Ringing upward, that plaint so mild :

"Oh God, how pale thy cheeks, my child !"

Fürwahr, ich glaube, wenn ich liege

Einst auf der schwarzen Todtenwiege,

Wo mich kein Menschenlaut mag stören—

Ich werde noch die stillen, bangen

Und vorwurfsvollen Worte hören:

O Gott, wie blaß sind deine Wangen!

Moritz Hartmann.

When 'tis decreed that I must die,

Upon the shrouded bier do lie,

Where human sounds disturb no more—

I know I'll hear those plaintive, mild,

Reproachful words, ay, as of yore:

"Oh God, how pale thy cheeks, my child!"

MORITZ HARTMANN.

Du bist die herrlichste von Allen.

Du bist die herrlichste von Allen,

So sonder Falsch, so schön und rein,

Ein Stern, vom Himmel frisch gefallen,

Er könnte selbst nicht schöner sein.

Du bist ein stilles, liebverklärtes

Gemüth, von Kindessinn beseelt,

Und das Bewußtsein deines Werthes

Die einz'ge Tugend, die dir fehlt.

Felix Dahn.

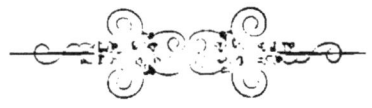

THOU ART THE PUREST ONE OF ALL.

THOU art the purest one of all,
    So gentle, kind, from falseness free,
Were from the Heav'ns a star to fall,
More beautiful it could not be!

Thou'rt like an angel sent to earth
On mission kind, that mission—*love;*
'Didst thou but know thy priceless worth,
Wouldst then be, e'en as they above!

FELIX DAHN.

Heimweh.

 laßt mich schlafen! o ruft mich
In die Gegenwart nicht zurück!
Mißgönnt ihr dem kranken Mädchen
Den Traum, den Schatten von Glück?

Was sprecht ihr mir zu? vergebens!
Mein Herz verstehet euch nicht.
Bin fremd in eurem Lande;
Hier schmerzt mich das Tageslicht.

Hier dehnt sich das flache Gefilde
So unabsehbar und leer,
Darüber legt sich der Himmel
So freud-und farblos und schwer.

HOME-SICKNESS.

CALL me not back to the present.

   Oh, let me sleep and dream,

Would you take from the broken-
   hearted,
Of joy the only gleam ?

Why speak to me ?   Not knoweth

My heart what you would say,

I'm in your land a·stranger,

Here pains the light of day.

Here so flat the plain extendeth

As far as the eye can see,

'Tis covered so dead and cheerless

By Heaven's canopy.

Es sieht mein müdes Auge,

Umflort von bitterm Thau,

Nur blasse Nebelgestalten,

Verschwindende, grau in grau.

Es rauschen fremde Klänge

Vorüber an meinem Ohr,

Es zählet die innere Stimme

Nur Schmerzen und Schmerzen mir vor.

Der Schlaf nur bringt allnächtlich

Vor Tagesgedanken mir Ruh',

Es trägt mich der Traum mitleidig

Der lieben Heimath zu.

My eye from weeping weary,

Discerneth far away

Nothing but airy visions,

Disappearing gray in gray.

Strange sounds I'm ever hearing,

Alas! a sad refrain;

My inner voice relateth

Alone of pain and pain.

Slumber alone brings rest me

From the bitter thoughts of day,

To home, sweet home in pity

My dreams take me away;

Und meine Berge erheben

Die schneeigen Häupter zumal,

Und tauchen in dunkele Bläue,

Und glühen im Morgenstrahl,

Und lauschen über den Hochwald,

Der schirmend die Gletscher umspannt,

In unser Thal herüber,

Und schauen mich an so bekannt.

Der Gießbach schäumet und brauset,

Und stürzt in die Schlucht sich hinab ;

Von drüben erschallt das Alphorn,—

Das ist der Hirtenknab !

And proudly lift my mountains

Their peaks bedecked with snow;

To the blue of Heaven looming,

In the morning light they glow.

They're frowning o'er the forest,

That girds the glaciers cold,

Into our lovely valley,

And greet me as of old.

The torrent of the Giesbach

From the rocky ridge doth fall;

The Alpine horn resoundeth

The shepherd's wonted call.

Aus unserm Hause tret' ich,

Dem zierlich gefügten, herfür;

Die Eltern haben's gebauet*),

Die Namen stehn über der Thür;

Und unter den Namen stehet

Der Spruch : Gott segne das Haus

Und segne, die frommen Gemüthes

Darin gehn ein und aus.

Ich bin hinausgegangen—

Weh' mir, daß ich es that!

Ich bin nun eine Waise,

Die keine Heimath hat.

---

*) Eigentlich „g e b a u e n ," welche Lesart ich die Schweizer und die, welche die Schweiz kennen, in den Text aufnehmen bitte.

And before our dear old cottage

I am standing as of yore;

My parents once did build it,

Their names are over the door.

And under their names is written:

"God bless this house for aye,

And bless all honest people

That pass this threshold may."

From its shelter once I wandered;

Through the world 'tis cold to roam:

I am now a weary orphan,

Without dear friends or home.

O laßt mich schlafen, o ruft mich

In die Gegenwart nicht zurück!

Mißgönnt nicht dem kranken Mädchen

Den Traum, den Schatten von Glück!

Adelbert von Chamiſſo.

Call me not back to the present,

Oh, let me sleep and dream,

Take not from the broken-hearted,

Of joy the only gleam!

ADELBERT VON CHAMISSO.

Herbstkummer.

Die Blumen vergehen,
　　Der Sommer ist hin,
Die Blätter verwehen,
Das trübt mir den Sinn.
Ein Röslein, das bracht' ich
Im Sommer in's Haus.
Es hält ja, so dacht' ich,
Den Winter wohl aus.

Die Vöglein sangen,
Es lauschte der Hain;
Die Rehlein, sie sprangen
Im Mondenschein.
Der Blümlein so viel hier
Erblühten im Thal,
Von allen gefiel mir
Das Röslein zumal.

AUTUMNAL-SORROW.

THE flowers are dead,
    Sweet Summer took flight,
The leaflets turn red,
And I mourn at the sight.
Last Summer I brought
A rose in my room.
'Twill keep, so I thought,
Through Winter's dark gloom.

The birdlings did sing
Through the listening vale;
The deer too did spring
In the moonlight pale.
Many flow'rs all around
I saw blooming so fair:
But not one, that I found,
With my *rose* could compare.

Der Herbst ist gekommen,

Der Sturm braust heran,

Die Luft ist verglommen,

Der Winter begann.

Gern wollt' ich nicht klagen

Um Stürme und Schnee,

Könnt's Röslein vertragen

Das eisige Weh.

O, schon' mir die Zarte,

Das liebliche Kind!

Die Eiche, die harte,

Umbrause, du Wind!

Blüh,' Röslein. ohn' Bangen,

Von Liebe gewacht,

Bis Winter bergangen.

Und Mai wieder lacht.

Ernst.

Then Autumn so drear
With its storms did begin;
All joys disappear,
And Winter sets in.
Complain I would ne'er
Of storms, or of snow,
If my *rose* could but bear
The icy woe.—

Oh, spare the sweet child,
Wind, thee I invoke!
Canst howl 'round the wild,
The sturdy oak!
Love watcheth thee, rose;
Canst bloom without fear,
Spite of storms and of snows,
Until May doth appear.

ERNST.

Sonnenblicke.

Kleine Blume im engen Thal,
　　Dich auch fand der Sonne Strahl,
Armes Herz in der kranken Brust,
Dir auch ward der Liebe Lust.

Und die Blume das Köpfchen hing,
Als die Sonne weiter ging,
Und das Herz, es brach entzwei,
Als das kurze Glück vorbei!

Albert Träger.

SUN-GLANCES.

ITTLE flower in valley green,

    Thee, too, found the sun's bright

    sheen,

Thou, poor heart in aching breast,

Too didst feel of love the zest.

But the flower soon hung its head,

When the sunlight onward sped,

And the heart did break in two,

When away love's pleasures flew.

ALBERT TRAEGER.

Zuflucht.

Thut man Kindern was zu Leide,
Fliehn zur Mutter sie voll Schrecken,
Sich in ihrem Faltenkleide
Vor dem Quäler zu verstecken.

Weiche Herzen bleiben Kinder
All ihr Leben, und es falle
Ihnen auch das Loos gelinder,
Als den Herzen von Metalle.

Jagt sie Unglück, wie zum Fluche,
Fliehn sie bang und immer bänger,
Bis sie hinterm Leichentuche
Sich verbergen ihrem Dränger.

Lenau.

REFUGE.

WHEN we children tease and worry,
 They from us attempt to hide,
Frightened to the mother hurry,
Finding refuge at her side.

Gentle hearts are children ever,
Little griefs they sorely feel;
They can bear their burdens never
Like those hardened hearts of steel.

Hunted down by ills tormenting,
Frightened more and more they fleet,
Till they hide from unrelenting
Foes, beneath the winding sheet.

LENAU.

Der Liebe Dauer.

lieb', so lang' du lieben kannst!

O lieb', so lang' du lieben magst!

Die Stunde kommt, die Stunde kommt,

Wo du an Gräbern stehst und klagst!

Und sorge, daß dein Herze glüht

Und Liebe hegt und Liebe trägt,

So lang' ihm noch ein ander Herz

In Liebe warm entgegenschlägt!

Und wer dir seine Brust erschließt,

O thu' ihm, was du kannst, zu Lieb'!

Und mach' ihm jede Stunde froh,

Und mach' ihm keine Stunde trüb!

LOVE'S DURATION.

Ⅱ love as long as thou canst love!
   Love in thy heart forever keep!
The hour will come, the hour will come,
When at the grave thou'lt kneel and weep.

See that thy heart doth warmly glow
With love, and let it no one rob,
So long another loving heart
In unison with thine doth throb.

Whoever doth confide in thee,
With roses strew life's rugged way!
For him make happy every hour,
Let no dark cloud between you stay !

Und hüte deine Zunge wohl,

Bald ist ein böses Wort gesagt!

O Gott, es war nicht bös gemeint,—

Der Andre aber geht und klagt.

O lieb', so lang' du lieben kannst!

O lieb', so lang' du lieben magst!

Die Stunde kommt, die Stunde kommt,

Wo du an Gräbern stehst und klagst!

Dann kniest du nieder an der Gruft,

Und birgst die Augen, trüb' und naß,

—Sie seh'n den Andern nimmermehr—

In's lange, feuchte Kirchhofsgras.

Guard well thy tongue, Oh, guard it well!

'Tis uttered soon, a word that pains—

"My God, I meant no harm!" But he

Is hurt and grievously complains.

Oh love as long as thou canst love!

Love in thy heart forever keep!

The hour will come, the hour will come,

When at the grave thou'lt kneel and weep.

And on the grave thou'lt kneel so sad,

Wilt hide thy tearful eyes (alas!

Those eyes will see him nevermore.)

Wilt hide them in the churchyard grass.

Und sprichst: O schau' auf mich herab,

Der hier an deinem Grabe weint!

Vergib, daß ich gekränkt dich hab'!

O Gott, es war nicht bös gemeint!

Er aber sieht und hört dich nicht,

Kommt nicht, daß du ihn froh umfängst:

Der Mund, der oft dich küßte, spricht

Nie wieder: ich vergab dir längst!

Er that's, vergab dir lange schon,

Doch manche heiße Thräne fiel

Um dich und um dein herbes Wort—

Doch still—er ruht, er ist am Ziel!

With trembling lips thou'lt cry : "Look
   down
On me, remorse my soul doth fill!

Forgive that I have pained thee so !

Oh God, I meant no harm, no ill ! "

He'll see and hear thee nevermore,

Thy arms canst not around him throw;

The mouth that kissed thee speaks no
   more:

"Oh, I forgave thee *long* ago!"

He did forgive thee long ago,

Though many a secret tear he shed

For thee, caused by that cank'ring word,

But hush—he slumbers with the dead.

O lieb', so lang' du lieben kannst!

O lieb', so lang' du lieben magst!

Die Stunde kommt, die Stunde kommt,

Wo du an Gräbern stehst und klagst!

Ferdinand Freiligrath.

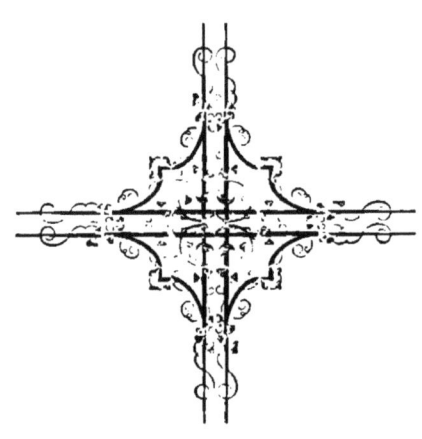

Oh love as long as thou canst love!

Love in thy heart forever keep!

The hour will come, the hour will come,

When at the grave thou'lt kneel and weep.

FERDINAND FREILIGRATH.

Waldgespräch.

Es ist schon spät, es wird schon kalt
 Was reitst du einsam durch den
 Wald?
Der Wald ist lang, du bist allein,
Du schöne Braut! Ich führ' dich heim!

„Groß ist der Männer Trug und List,
Vor Schmerz mein Herz gebrochen ist,
Wohl irrt das Waldhorn her und hin,
O flieh! du weißt nicht, wer ich bin.“

So reich geschmückt ist Roß und Weib,
So wunderschön der junge Leib,
Jetzt kenn' ich dich—Gott steh' mir bei!
Du bist die Hexe Lorelei.

FOREST-TALK.

IT is so late, it cold hath grown,

Why through the woods dost ride
alone

So late at night, on such a ride.

I'll lead thee home, my pretty bride!

" Men's artful ways are many, pain

My heart hath broken, torn in twain ;

The forest horn sounds far and near,

Away! thou'lt know me but to fear."

The steed is decked so wondrous fine,

The rider looks so fair, divine ;—

Protect me God! I know thee now,

The witch, Oh, Lorelei art thou!

„Du kennst mich wohl,—von hohem Stein

Schaut still mein Schloß tief in den Rhein.

Es ist schon spät, es wird schon kalt,

Kommst nimmermehr aus diesem Wald!"

Joseph Baron von Eichendorff.

"I am, on cliffs my castle stands,

A view of 'Father Rhine' commands.

It is so late, it cold doth grow,

From hence thou nevermore wilt go!"

JOSEPH BARON VON EICHENDORFF.

Am Fenster.

Sitzt die Mutter mit der schönen Tochter

An dem Fenster in der Abendkühle,

Geht ein junger Wandersmann vorüber,

Blickt verstohlen nach dem hohen Fenster,

Und sein Auge trifft ein andres Auge,

Und wie Purpur glühen seine Wangen

Und ein Zauber hemmet seinen Schritt.

Und zur Mutter spricht die Tochter hastig:

„Wie ist's doch so schwül noch in dem Zimmer!"

Und sie eilet nach dem nächsten Fenster,

Wo auf reichgeschmücktem Blumenbrete

Eine duft'ge Rose sich erschlossen.

AT THE WINDOW.

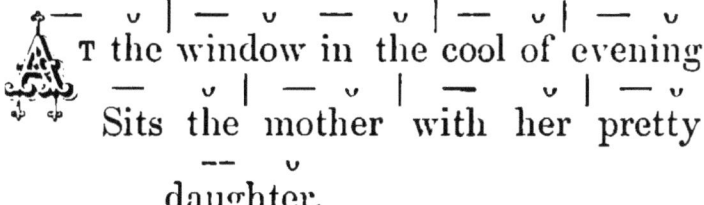

At the window in the cool of evening

Sits the mother with her pretty

daughter,

Lo, there passeth by a youthful wand'rer,

Throwing stealthy glances at the window,

And his eye another eye there meeteth,

And his burning cheeks do glow like pur-
ple,

And some wonder seems to hem his step.

To her mother quickly speaks the daugh-
ter:

"Oh, how close 'tis in the room, dear
mother!"

And she speedeth to the nearest window,

Where, upon a flow'r-stand richly gar-
nished,

Just a fragrant rosebud had expanded.

Und sie öffnet mit Geräusch das Fenster,

Bengt sich weit hinaus und ruft erschrocken:

„Mütterlein, ach wirst du mir nicht zürnen,

Meine Rose, meine schöne Rose,

Die du mir am Namenstage schenktest

Und die heut' so lieblich sich erschlossen,

Hab' ich Ungeschickte abgebrochen.

Wäre sie nur nicht hinabgefallen,

Blühte sie mir lange noch im Glase.

Aber sieh! dort hat sie schon ein Fremder

Eilig von der Straße aufgehoben

Und mit ihr den Wanderhut geschmückt."

Und sie küßt die Hand der Mutter schmeichelnd

Und es ruht der Mutter Auge selig

And with noise she openeth wide the
    window,
Leaneth out, and starting back exclaim-
    eth:
"Wilt thou not be angry with me, mother?

For my rose, my rose so fondly treasured,

Given me by thee upon my birth-day,

Which to-day its lovely folds had opened,

Broke I from its branch, so awkward.

If it only had not fallen downward,

In a vase for days I might have kept it.

But behold—a passing stranger yonder,

From the street alas! hath quickly picked it,

And his hat it gaily now adorneth."

And her mother tenderly she kisseth,

And her mother's eye enchanted resteth

Auf dem schönen Kind und tröstend spricht sie:

„Sollt' ich wegen einer Rose zürnen?

Mag der Wanderer sich ihrer freuen,

Der vielleicht, der lieben Heimath denkend,

In der Rose, die ein wildes Mädchen

Wider Willen ihm hinabgesendet,

Einen Gruß sieht, den sein theures Liebchen

Nach ihm ausgesandt in ferne Lande.

Wie! noch immer glühen deine Wangen?

Und nun Thränen gar noch in dem Auge?

Ei, so tröste dich doch nur, mein Kindchen!

Morgen schenk' ich dir ein andres Röschen,

Viel noch sah ich bei dem Gärtner stehn."

Und die Tochter birgt ihr weinend Antlitz

On her pretty child, and she consoleth:

" Should a little rose cause me to anger ?

May it be a source of pleasure to the

Wand'rer, who perchance of sweet home
    thinking,
In the rose, which by a thoughtless maiden

Wayward, 'gainst intention hath been
    thrown him,
Doth a greeting see from his beloved,

Sent him to a far and distant country.

What, still on thy cheeks that heightened
    color ?
Even tears into thy eyes are creeping ?

Be consoled my pet, my darling daughter,

I will buy another rose thee shortly,

Many saw I at the florist's grow ! "

And the maiden hides her face yet weep-
    ing,

An der Mutter liebevollem Busen,

Und die Mutter kann es nicht begreifen,

Daß ihr wildes, ausgelass'nes Mädchen

Eines abgeknickten Rösleins willen

Gar so still und traurig ist.

Julius Sturm.

On her mother's kind and loving breast.

Sore perplexed and greatly puzzled is the

Mother, that her cheerful daughter, for a

Little broken rose's sake, should ever

Be so serious, mournful, still.

JULIUS STURM.

Das Todtenhemdchen.

Starb das Kindlein.
    Ach, die Mutter
Saß am Tag und weinte, weinte,
Saß zur Nacht und weinte.

Da erscheint das Kindlein wieder,
In dem Todtenhemd, so blaß;
Sagt zur Mutter: „Leg' dich nieder!
Sieh, mein Hemdchen
Wird von deinen lieben Thränen
Gar so naß,
Und ich kann nicht schlafen, Mutter!"

Und das Kind verschwindet wieder,
Und die Mutter weint nicht mehr.

Eduard von Bauernfeld.

THE LITTLE DEATH GOWN.

EAD the child is.
Oh! its mother
Sits all day and weepeth, weepeth,
Sits at night and weepeth.

Sadly in its little gown,
Now the child again appears;
Tells its mother: " Lie thee down,
See, my gown
Is so wet now, from thy bitter,
Loving tears;
And I cannot sleep, dear mother!"

And again it disappears,
But its mother weeps no more.

EDUARD VON BAUERNFELD.

Nachtigall und Rose.

Die Nachtigall.

Sang mit wundersüßem Schall
Also einst die Nachtigall:
„Wie so hold und wunderschön,
Rose, bist du anzusehn!
Blühend,
Glühend,
Düfte sprühend.
Weh! ich muß des Busens Dräng
Strömen aus in flücht'gem Klang,
Der mit Sangesallgewalt
Wonnig sich in Lüften wiegt,
Aber bald
Leis verhallt
Und verfliegt.

NIGHTINGALE AND ROSE.

The Nightingale.

SANG with sweetness in the vale,
Thus the pretty Nightingale :—
"Oh, so fair and wondrous sweet
Art thou, Rose, in thy retreat !
Blowing,
Glowing,
Fragrance throwing.
I, in what my heart abounds,
Must pour out in fleeting sounds,
Which are borne with mighty sway
On the wings of zephyrs light ;
Soon are they
Far away
In their flight.

Ach! was flüchtig stets verschallt,

Könnt' ich's fassen in Gestalt!

Dann entschwänden nicht im Nu

Klänge, die der Brust entsprangen;

Würden prangen

Schön, wie du,

Blühend,

Glühend,

Düfte sprühend,

Eine Ros' an Liedes Statt,

Jeder Ton ein Rosenblatt!

Rose, darum lieb' ich dich

Inniglich!"

Oh, that I, what will not stay,

Only could in form array !

Never then should cease, as now,

Sounds which swell this heart of mine :

They should shine

Bright, as thou,

Blowing,

Glowing,

Fragrance throwing.

Every note a leaf or spray,

Every song a rose of May !

Therefore, Rose, I love but thee

Heartily !"

Die Rose.

Rose gab mit duft'gem Weh'n

Leise flüsternd zu versteh'n:

„Ach! wie singst du, Nachtigall,

Mit so wunderholdem Schall!

Innig,

Minnig,

Süß und sinnig.

Was das Herz mir schwellt mit Macht,

Was mich hold erglühen macht,

Lebt im Duft mit Allgewalt,

Der in Lüften wonnig weht,

Aber bald

Leis entwallt

Und vergeht.

The Rose.

Rose then, wafting fragrance pure,

Softly whispered, shy, demure :—

"Oh, how sweetly, Nightingale,

Singest thou o'er hill and dale !

Clearly,

Dearly,

Sweet, sincerely.

That which fills me with delight,

That which makes me glow so bright,

Gently through the zephyr sighs,

Fades away,

'Twill not stay,

Soon it dies.

Ach! was ohne Klang entwallt,

Unerkannt, vergessen bald,

Was mit Macht die Brust durchzieht—

Könnt' ich's laut und freudig singen,

Würd' es klingen,

Wie dein Lied,

Innig,

Minnig,

Süß und sinnig.

Düfte—Nachtigallgesang,

Jeder Athemzug ein Klang!

Nachtigall, ich liebe dich

Inniglich!"

Friedrich von Sallet.

What is born without a tone,

Soon forgotten, hardly known,

What my heart to please is fain :—

Could I loud and clear it sing,

It should ring

Like thy strain,

Clearly,

Dearly,

Sweet, sincerely.

Fragrance—song of Nightingale

Warbling over hill and dale!

Nightingale, I love but thee

Heartily!"

FRIEDRICH VON SALLET.

Einſt.

Wir ſtanden vor einem Grabe,
    Umweht von Fliederduft;
Still mit den Gräſeſ : des Hügels
Spielte die Abendluft.

Da ſprach ſie bang' und leiſe:
„Wenn von der Welt ich ſchied,
Und kaum mein Angedenken
Noch lebt in deinem Lied;

Wenn du auf weiter Erde
Verlaſſen und einſam biſt,
Und nur im Traum der Nächte
Mein Geiſt dich leiſe küßt:

ONCE.

T a grave we stood; sweet fragrance filled
The silent woodland ground,
And softly played the evening air, with
The grasses of the mound.

With trembling lip she whispered then:
"Should I from thee e'er part,
Doth scarce a thought of me more live
Yet in thy songful heart;

"If in the cold, wide world thou art
Forsaken, treated ill,
And only in thy dreams at night
My soul doth kiss thee still;

Dann komm zu meinem Grabe,

Von Flieder und Rosen umlaubt,

Und neig' auf die kühlen Gräser

Das heiße, müde Haupt.

Ein Sträußchen duftiger Blumen

Bringst du als sonst mir mit;

Mich weckt aus tiefem Schlummer

Dein lieber bekannter Schritt.

Dann will ich mit dir flüstern

So heimlich und vertraut,

Wie damals, wo wir innig

In's Aug' uns noch geschaut.

" Then to my grave do quickly come,

O'er-run with vine and rose,

And on the cool, refreshing grass,

Thy weary head repose.

"A nosegay sweet, as thou wert wont,

Oh, bring with thee, my own !

From slumber then will waken me

Thy step, the dear, well-known.

"And I will whisper gently, soft,

Confidingly with thee,

As thrilled with love we often did,

Ere Death did summon me.

Und wer vorübergehet,

Der denkt: es ist der Wind,

Der durch die Blüthen des Flieders

Hinsäuselt leis und lind.

Und wie du lebst, das Kleinste

Berichten sollst du mir,

Und ich will dir erzählen,

Was ich geträumt von dir.

Wenn dann der Abend gekommen

Und Stern an Stern erwacht,

Dann wünschen wir uns leise

Und heimlich: gute Nacht.

"And whosoever passeth by

Will think: ' It is I trow,

The wind that rustles through the leaves

So sweetly and so low.'

" What thou hast done, Oh, tell it all!

Though trifling it may seem,

And I will gladly let thee know

What I of thee did dream.

"When evening throws her mantle 'round,

And stars the Heaven light,

Then we will bid each other still

And lovingly, good night.

Du gehst getröstet nach Hause

Im Abenddämmerschein,

Und unter meinen Blumen

Schlaf' still ich wieder ein."

Eduard Ferrand.

" Thou goest home, of pain relieved,

The stars thy path illume,

And I again then fall asleep

Beneath my flowery tomb."

EDUARD FERRAND.

Perlenfischer.

Du liebes Auge, willst dich tauchen

In meines Aug's geheimste Tiefe,

Zu spähen, wo in blauen Gründen

Verborgen eine Perle schliefe?

Du liebes Auge, tauche nieder,

Und in die klare Tiefe dringe,

Und lächle, wenn ich dir dein Bildniß

Als schönste Perle wiederbringe!

Otto Roquette.

THE PEARL-FISHER.

WILT dive, thou lovely eye, wilt dive
    Into my eye's most hidden deep,
To spy where in this deepness blue,
Secreted well, a pearl doth sleep?

Oh, do dive down, thou lovely eye,
And penetrate the deepness clear,
And smile, if it thy image doth
Reflect, as pearl most fine, most dear.

OTTO ROQUETTE.

Primula veris.

I.

ieblidje Blume,
    Bift du fo früh fdjon
Wiedergefommen?
Sei mir gegrüßet,
Primula veris!

Leifer denn alle
Blumen der Wiefe
Haft du gefdjlummert,
Liebliche Blume,
Primula veris!

Dir nur vernehmbar
Lockte das erfte
Sanfte Geflüfter
Weckenden Frühlings,
Primula veris!

PRIMULA-VERIS.

(The Primrose.)

I.

OVELY flower,
Art thou so early
Once more among us?
Fondly I greet thee,
Primula Veris!

Lighter than all the
Meadow's fair flowers,
Gently didst slumber,
Lovely flower,
Primula Veris!

Only perceived by
Thee, the first gentle
Whisp'rings of wak'ning
Spring, did entice thee,
Primula Veris!

Mir auch im Herzen

Blühte vor Zeiten,

Schöner denn alle

Blumen der Liebe,

Primula veris!

II.

Liebliche Blume,

Primula veris!

Holde, dich nenn' ich

Blume des Glaubens.

Gläubig dem ersten

Winke des Himmels

Eilst du entgegen,

Oeffnest die Brust ihm.

Once in my heart so
Sweetly was blooming,
Brighter than all the
Flowers of Cupid,
Primula Veris !

II.

Lovely flower,
Primula Veris,
Flower of Faith, I
Wondering call thee; ..

Heaven's first glance thou,
Trusting with fervor,
Speedest to meet, e'en
Open'st thy breast to't.

Frühling ist kommen.

Mögen ihn Fröste,

Trübende Nebel

Wieder verhüllen;

Blume, du glaubst es,

Daß der ersehnte

Göttliche Frühling

Endlich gekommen,

Oeffnest die Brust ihm;

Aber es dringen

Lauernde Fröste

Tödtlich ins Herz dir.

Spring now appeareth,

Although the nipping

Frosts, and the dreary

Fogs may revail it——

Flower, *thou* believest,

That the long wished for

Heavenly Spring, hath

Made its appearance.

Open'st thy breast to't;

Wounded thy heart is,

Frosts that are painful,

Fatal, have pierced it.

Mag es verwelken!

Ging doch der Blume

Gläubige Seele

Nimmer verloren!

Lenau.

Though it may wither,

Still the bright flower's

Spirit so faithful,

Never can perish.

LENAU.

Der Preis.

Es ist kein hoher Berg so hoch,
    So tief kein tiefes Thal,
Es dringt hinauf ein Vögelein,
Hinab ein Sonnenstrahl.

Und wärst du selbst die Perl' im Meer
Und wärst das Abendgold,
So hoch und tief hätt' ich dein Herz,
Kostbares Kind, geholt.

J. G. Fischer.

THE PRICE.

WHERE is no mount however high,
    No vale however deep,
But that to it a bird can fly,
On it the sun can peep.

And wert thou e'en the evening sky,
In sea the pearl so fair,
Thy heart I should have won thus high,
Thus low, no matter where.

J. G. FISCHER.

Blick in den Strom.

Sahst du ein Glück vorübergehn,

Das nie sich wiederfindet,

Ist's gut in einen Strom zu sehn,

Wo Alles wogt und schwindet.

O, starre nur hinein, hinein,

Du wirst es leichter missen,

Was dir, und soll's dein Liebstes sein,

Vom Herzen ward gerissen.

Blick' unverwandt hinab zum Fluß,

Bis deine Thränen fallen,

Und sieh durch ihren warmen Guß

Die Flut hinunterwallen.

GAZE INTO THE STREAM.*

Saw'st thou a joy fade like a dream,
Not to return, alas?
'Tis well to gaze into a stream,
Where all doth swell and pass.

Oh stare into the waters, stare!
What from thy heart was wrest,
The loss thereof canst better bear,
Though thou didst love it best.

Gaze in the stream, turn not thy head
'Till tear doth fall on tear,
And through this torrent warmly shed,
The flood watch disappear.

---

* This lay, than which there exists none imbued with deeper poetical feeling, was conceived Sept. 15th, 1844, on the river Danube; it was written Sept. 25th, 1844, but a few days previous to the author's sad and fatal malady.

Hinträumend wird Vergessenheit

Des Herzens Wunde schließen;

Die Seele sieht mit ihrem Leid

Sich selbst vorüberfließen.

Lenau.

Oblivion, as thou dream'st, will close

Thy heart's deep wound, and ay,

Thy soul will see, with all its woes,

Itself a passing by !

LENAU.

An den Sonnenschein.

Sonnenschein! o Sonnenschein!

Wie scheinst du mir in's Herz hinein!

Weckst drinnen lauter Liebeslust,

Daß mir so enge wird die Brust!

Und enge wird mir Stub' und Haus,

Und wie ich lauf' zum Thor hinaus,

Da lockst du gar in's frische Grün

Die allerschönsten Mädchen hin!

O Sonnenschein! du glaubest wohl,

Daß ich wie du es machen soll,

Der jede schmucke Blume küßt,

Die eben nur sich dir erschließt?

TO THE SUNBEAM.

H, sunbeam, merry sunbeam thou!

How in my heart thou shinest now!

Dost wake therein love's brightest dreams,

So that my heart too narrow seems!

My room and house so narrow grow,

And when outside the gate* I go,

Enticest thou to meadows green,

Behold! the fairest maidens e'en.

Dost think no doubt, Oh, sunbeam bright!

To act like thee for me 'twere right :

Thou kissest all the flowers free,

That dare to ope their folds to thee.

---

*Walled towns have gates on different sides, that communicate with the open country.

Haſt doch ſo lang' die Welt erblickt,

Und weißt, daß ſich's für mich nicht ſchickt ;

Was machſt du mir denn ſolche Pein ?

O Sonnenſchein ! o Sonnenſchein !

Robert Reinick.

Upon the world hast gazed so long,

And knowest well for me 'twere wrong;

Oh, wherefore then, dost pain me now,

Oh, merry, merry sunbeam thou!

ROBERT REINICK.

Das Kind.

Sie Mutter lag im Todtenschrein,

 Zum letzten Mal geschmückt;

Da spielt das kleine Kind herein,

Das staunend sie erblickt.

Die Blumenkron' im blonden Haar

Gefällt dem Kindlein sehr,

Die Busenblumen, bunt und klar,

Zum Strauß geweiht, noch mehr.

Und sanft und schmeichelnd ruft es aus

Du liebe Mutter, gib

Mir eine Blum' aus deinem Strauß,

Ich hab' dich auch so lieb!

THE CHILD.

x death's cold bier the mother lay
  In garments pure and white,
Her little child comes full of play
And wonders at the sight.

Those roses in her golden hair,
The child, with joy do fill;
On bosom cold, the flowers fair,
Do please it, ay, more still.

It calls in tones caressing, mild,
"Mother, dear mother, pray,
A flower give thy darling child,
But one, from thy bouquet!"

Und als die Mutter es nicht thut,

Da denkt das Kind für sich:

Sie schläft, doch wenn sie ausgeruht,

So thut sie's sicherlich.

Schleicht fort, so leis' es immer kann,

Und schließt die Thüre sacht,

Und lauscht von Zeit zu Zeit daran,

Ob Mutter noch nicht wacht.

Friedrich Hebbel.

But since no sound the silence breaks,

It thinks and whispers low :

" Dear mother sleeps, when she awakes,

She'll give it me, I know ! "

On tiptoe then it quits the bier,

Her slumber not to break,

And comes from time to time, to hear

If mother's not awake.

FRIEDRICH HEBBEL.

Die Rose.

Und als die Nachtigall geendet
Im Lindenbaum ihr schönstes Lied,
Da ist in heil'ger Morgenstunde
Die rothe Rose aufgeblüht.

Und trunken von dem Morgengolde,
Das durch die grünen Ranken fällt,
Grüßt sie mit schauerndem Erröthen
Zum ersten Mal die Gotteswelt.

Da zittert in dem goldnen Auge
Wohl eine Perle silberrein:
Es soll der Dank der schönen Blume
Für ihren Himmelsschöpfer sein.

THE ROSE.

ND when the nightingale had finished,

In the linden tree its sweetest lay,

Then at the holy hour of morning,

The red rose woke to light of day.

And by the rays of morn elated,

That creep through twigs and leaflets green,

It shyly greets, with many blushes,

The world of God for first time seen.

Now in its golden eye doth tremble

A pearl so silver-like and clear;

It is the praise the flower offers

Up to the Lord, in higher sphere.

Und alle Zauber zu vollenden,

Ward ihr auf ros'ge Stirn geküßt

Das holde, reizende Geheimniß:

Daß sie nicht weiß, wie schön sie ist.

Ferdinand Stolle.

And to complete this charming wonder,

Lo, Nature on its brow doth kiss

The sweet and all enchanting secret,

Of knowing not how sweet it is.

FERDINAND STOLLE.

Die Thräne.

Im Winter, wo die Welt ringsher
    So schauerlich erblichen,
Ist eine Thräne trüb' und schwer
In's Auge mir geschlichen.

Die Welt erwacht aus ihrem Tod,
Der Winter ist vertrieben!
Ich rieb mein Auge feuerroth,
Die Thräne ist geblieben.

Vergebens wird auf Baum und Flur
Sein Gold der Frühling sticken,
Ich soll die blühende Natur
In Thränen nur erblicken.

THE TEAR.

IN Winter deep, when faded, sere

And cold the world had grown,

There crept into my eye a tear,

So still and unbeknown :

The world again to life returns,

And gone are Winter's pains ;

I rub my eye, e'en till it burns,

Alas! the tear remains.

For naught will Spring the field and tree

With gorgeous lustre clad,

For blooming Nature I dare see

Alone through tears so sad.

Im Winter gab es böse Zeit,

Da dacht' ich oft so trübe

Der seligen Vergangenheit,

So voll von Glück und Liebe.

Dann dacht' ich, was ich all' gestrebt

Und was mir all' mißlungen,

Und wie ich ewig gluthbelebt,

Doch nie ein Ziel errungen.

Ich dachte, wie es schmerzt und brennt,

Dies ewig leere Streben :

Mein Denken war ein Monument

Auf ein verfehltes Leben.

Oh, Winter with its pains did blast

All hopes, then thought I of

The dear old times, the happy past,

So full of joy and love.

I thought of all I strove to do,

How little did attain ;

And how when failing, strove anew,

But all alas ! in vain.

I thought how fruitless strivings smart

And burn——a monument

My thinking was, to an aching heart,

To my poor life mis-spent.

Mein Fühlen war so öd' und leer,

Und alles Glück entwichen;

Da ist die Thräne trüb' und schwer

In's Auge mir geschlichen.

Carl Ferd: Dräxler=Manfred.

My thoughts became so sad and drear

And all my joys had flown:

Then crept into my eye the tear,

So still and unbeknown.

O. F. DRAEXLER-MANFRED.

Die Sennin.

Schöne Sennin, noch einmal
　　Singe deinen Ruf in's Thal,
Daß die frohe Felsensprache
Deinem hellen Ruf erwache.

Horch, o Mädchen, wie dein Sang
In die Brust den Bergen drang,
Wie dein Wort die Felsenseelen
Freudig fort und fort erzählen!

Aber einst, wie Alles flieht,
Scheidest du mit deinem Lied,
Wenn dich Liebe fortbewogen,
Oder dich der Tod entzogen.

THE ALPINE SHEPHERDESS.

MAIDEN, sing thy sweet refrain
   In the valley once again,
That the mountains' language dear
Wake upon thy call so clear.

List, Oh maiden, how thy song
Thro' the mountains' breast doth throng,
How they one another tell,
Pleased, the words they love so well.

But alas ! as all will die,
With thy song thou too wilt fly;
When away by Love persuaded,
Or thy heart by Death invaded.

Und verlaffen werden ftehn,

Traurig ftumm herüberfehn

Dort die grauen Felfenzinnen

Und auf deine Lieder finnen.

Lenau.

And forsaken then will stand,

Gazing silent in the land,

Yonder snow-capped peaks, and long

Sadly for thy merry song.

LENAU.

An den Wind.

Ich wandre fort in's ferne Land;
    Noch einmal blickt' ich um, bewegt,
Und sah, wie sie den Mund geregt,
Und wie gewinket ihre Hand.

Wohl rief sie noch ein freundlich Wort
Mir nach auf meinen trüben Gang,
Doch hört' ich nicht den liebsten Klang,
Weil ihn der Wind getragen fort.

Daß ich mein Glück verlassen muß,
Du rauher, kalter Windeshauch,
Ist's nicht genug, daß du mir auch
Entreißest ihren letzten Gruß?

Lenau.

TO THE WIND.

WANDER forth in foreign land ;
Once more I turned, with heavy heart,
And saw yet that her lips did part,
And that she waved her lily hand.

No doubt she sent some greeting kind
To me, upon my journey drear;
The lovely sound I could not hear,
For it was stifled by the wind.

That I must leave my Love so true,
Is it not sad, Oh, not enough,
Thou cruel wind, so cold and rough,
That yet must rob her last adieu?

BENAU.

Wenn du willst im Menschenherzen.

Wenn du willst im Menschenherzen
Alle Saiten rühren an,
Stimme du den Ton der Schmerzen,
Nicht den Klang der Freuden an.

Mancher ist wohl, der erfahren
Hat auf Erden keine Lust;
Keiner, der nicht still bewahren
Wird ein Weh in seiner Brust.

Friedrich Rückert.

WOULD YOU HEAR A HEART'S REFRAIN?

WOULD you hear a heart's refrain,

    When its strings are all in play?

Touch the chords of bitter pain,

Never those of pleasure, pray.

Many happy ones are there,

Who on earth no pleasures know;

None, who've carried meekly ne'er,

In their breast some silent woe.

FRIEDRICH RUECKERT.

Die sterbende Blume.

Hoffe! du erlebst es noch,
    Daß der Frühling wiederkehrt.
Hoffen alle Bäume doch,
Die des Herbstes Wind verheert,
Hoffen mit der stillen Kraft
Ihrer Knospen winterlang,
Bis sich wieder regt der Saft,
Und ein neues Grün entsprang.

„Ach, ich bin kein starker Baum,
Der ein Sommertausend lebt,
Nach verträumtem Wintertraum
Neue Lenzgedichte webt!
Ach, ich bin die Blume nur,
Die des Maies Kuß geweckt.
Und von der nicht bleibt die Spur,
Wie das weiße Grab sie deckt!"—

THE DYING FLOWER.

HOPE, for thou wilt live to see
  Spring again return so fair!
Hopeth not ay, every tree,
Chilled though by autumnal air?
Through the Winter bleak and hoar,
Hope its buds, and have no fears,
'Till the sap doth rise once more
And a verdure fresh appears.

"I'm no sturdy tree that lasts
Thousand Summers, the forest's king,
Dreams 'mid Winter's chilling blasts,
Wakes to weave new songs of Spring:
I'm the little flower bright,
Brought to light by kiss of May,
Once beneath my grave so white,
I, alas! must sleep for aye.

Wenn du denn die Blume bist,

O bescheidenes Gemüth,

Tröste dich, beschieden ist

Samen Allem, was da blüht.

Laß den Sturm des Todes doch

Deinen Lebensstaub verstreu'n.

Aus dem Staube wirst du noch

Hundertmal dich selbst erneu'n.—

„Ja, es werden nach mir blüh'n

Andre, die mir ähnlich sind ;

Ewig ist das ganze Grün,

Nur das Einzle welkt geschwind.

Aber, sind sie, was ich war,

Bin ich selber es nicht mehr ;

Jetzt nur bin ich ganz und gar,

Nicht zuvor und nicht nachher.

Art the flow'ret, thou, indeed,

Modest being, then do know,

Be consoled,—there is decreed

Seed for all that e'er doth grow.

Scattered let thy *life's* dust be

By the storms of death, be told

From that dust renewed thou'lt see

Soon thyself an hundred fold.

" True 'tis, after me will glow

Others like me, frail and shy;

Verdure doth forever grow,

But the single leaf must die.

Though they be what *I* was, *thou*

Knowest *I* am it no more;

I am living only now,

Not hereaft and not before!

„Wenn einst sie der Sonne Blick
Wärmt, der jetzt noch mich durchflammt,
Lindert das nicht mein Geschick,
Das mich nun zur Nacht verdammt.
Sonne, ja du ängelst schon
Ihnen in die Fernen zu;
Warum noch mit frost'gem Hohn
Mir aus Wolken lächelst du?

„Weh' mir, daß ich dir vertraut,
Als mich wach geküßt dein Strahl:
Daß in's Aug' ich dir geschaut,
Bis es mir das Leben stahl!
Dieses Lebens armen Rest
Deinem Mitleid zu entziehn,
Schließen will ich krankhaft fest
Mich in mich, und dir entfliehn!

" When the sun doth shine so bright,

Warming them as it doth me,

I'll be doomed to endless night

By the curse of destiny.

In advance thou even now,

Sun, dost greet them warm and soft :

Why with frosty sneers dost thou

Smile on me from clouds aloft ?

"And I trusted thee on high,

When to life kissed by thy ray,

Gazed alas! into thy eye,

Till it stole my life away !

For my life's poor moments last,

I'll no mercy have from thee,

In myself I'll close me fast

And thy kiss forever flee.

„Doch du schmelzest meines Grimms

Starres Eis in Thränen auf;

Nimm mein fliehend Leben, nimm's,

Ewige, zu dir hinauf!

Ja, du sonnest noch den Gram

Aus der Seele mir zuletzt;

Alles, was von dir mir kam,

Sterbend dank' ich dir es jetzt:

„Aller Lüfte Morgenzug,

Dem ich sommerlang gebebt,

Aller Schmetterlinge Flug,

Die um mich im Tanz geschwebt;

Augen, die mein Glanz erfrischt,

Herzen, die mein Duft erfreut;

Wie aus Duft und Glanz gemischt

Du mich schufst, dir dank' ich's heut'.

"But the rigid ice of ire
Meltest thou to tears, behold!
Take my life, 'twill soon expire,
Up, eternal, to thy fold!
Thou wilt sun my grief, until
From my soul it taketh leave,
What I owe unto thy will,
For it all, my thanks receive!

" For the morning zephyrs light,
That did me all Summer kiss,
For the lepidopter's flight,
Hov'ring round me full of bliss;
For the eyes that I did charm,
For the hearts I did rejoice—
Dying I do thank thee warm,
And in praise do lift my voice!

„Eine Zierde deiner Welt,

Wenn auch eine kleine nur,

Ließest du mich blühn im Feld,

Wie die Stern' auf höh'rer Flur.

Einen Odem hauch' ich noch,

Und er soll kein Seufzer sein;

Einen Blick zum Himmel hoch,

Und zur schönen Welt hinein.

„Ew'ges Flammenherz der Welt,

Laß verglimmen mich an dir!

Himmel, spann' dein blaues Zelt,

Mein vergrüntes sinket hier.

Heil, o Frühling, deinem Schein!

Morgenluft, Heil deinem Wehn!

Ohne Kummer schlaf' ich ein,

Ohne Hoffnung, aufzustehn."

Friedrich Rückert.

"Of thy world a gem, although

But a little modest one,

Thou didst brightly let me glow

Like the stars on high, Oh Sun !

Dying now without a sigh,

Death, dread death, resigned I meet;

But one glance to Heaven high,

And one on the earth so sweet.

" Earth's eternal heart so true,

Heart of fire, to thee I fly !

Heaven span thy tent so blue,

Here my withered self doth die !

Hail thy waftings, morning air !

Hail sweet Spring, thy gorgeous ray !

I, sans sorrow, grief or care,

Fall asleep, though 'tis for aye ! "

FRIEDRICH RUZCKERT.

Wunsch.

Fort möcht' ich reisen
      Weit, weit in die See,
O meine Geliebte,
Mit dir allein!

Die Dränger und Lauscher
Und kalten Störer,
Sie hielt' uns ferne
Der wallende Abgrund,
Das drohende Meer,
Wir wären so sicher
Und selig allein.
Und käme der Sturm,
Ich würde dich halten
An meiner Brust.
Wenn donnernde Wogen

WISH.

FAIN would I travel
    Far over the sea,
Thou, my beloved,
With thee alone!

Intruders and list'ners,
And cold disturbers,
Would keep far distant
The surging abyss,
The threatening sea.
So safe we should be
And happy alone.
Were storms to come,
I'd clasp thee firmly
And close to my breast.
Were billows to thunder

Zum Himmel schlügen,

Doch höher schlüge

Mein trunkenes Herz;

Und meine Liebe,

Die ewige, starke,

Sie würde frohlockend

Dich halten im Sturm.

Du würdest zitternd

Mir blicken in's Auge,

Und würdest erblicken,

Was nimmer scheitert

In allen Stürmen,

Und würdest lächeln

Und nicht mehr zittern.

And leap up to Heaven,

Still higher would leap then

My joyful heart ;

And my love so faithful,

So true, eternal,

Would exultantly hold thee

While raged the storm.

Affrighted, trembling

Thou wouldst gaze in my eye, and

Thou wouldst behold there,

What wrecketh never

In storms severest,

And thou wouldst smile then,

And nevermore tremble.

Sieh, nun ermüdet

Der tobende Aufruhr,

In Schlummer sinken

Die Wellen und Winde,

Und über den Wassern

Ist tiefe Stille.

Da ruhst du sinnend

An meiner Brust.

So tiefe Stille :

Mein lauschendes Herz

Hört Antwort pochen

Dein lauschendes Herz.

Wir sind allein,

Doch flüsterst du leise,

Behold !—Now tires

The roaring commotion,

The waves and the winds are

Falling to slumber,

And over the waters

Tranquility reigns.

Thou restest thoughtful

Upon my breast.

So deep the stillness,

My listening heart

Hears answer throbbing

Thy listening heart.

Though we are alone,

The thoughtful Ocean

Um nicht zu stören

Das sinnende Meer.

Nur sanft erzittern

Die Lippen dir,

Die schwellenden Blätter

Der süßen Rose;

Ich sauge dein Wort,

Den klingenden Duft

Der süßen Rose.

Im Osten hebt sich

Der klare Mond,

Und Gott bedecket

Den Himmel mit Sternen,

Und ich bedecke,

Not to disturb, thou

Dost whisper gently,

And softly quiver

Only thy lips,—

The undulating

Leaves of the rose;

I drink in thy words,

The ringing fragrance

Of the lovely rose.

In the East now riseth

The moon so clear,

And God doth cover

With stars the Heaven,

And I do cover,

Selig wie er,

Dein liebes Antlitz,

Den schönern Himmel,

Mit feurigen Küssen.

Lenau.

Happy like Him,

Thy face so lovely,

The sweeter Heaven,

With fiery kisses.

LENAU.

Begrabe deine Todten.

Begrabe deine Todten
    Tief in dein Herz hinein;
So werden sie dein Leben
Lebend'ge Todte sein.

So werden sie im Herzen
Stets wieder auferstehn,
Als gute, lichte Engel
Mit dir durch's Leben gehn.

Begrab' dein eigen Leben
In Andrer Herz hinein;
So wirst du, und bist du ein Todter,
Ein ewig Lebender sein.

Carl Siebel.

THY DEAD, OH, BURY THEM.

Thy dead, Oh, bury them
 Deep in thy heart, ay deep;
For then, though dead, they'll live
'Till *thou* dost fall asleep!

Yea, in thy heart they'll rise
Again like angels pure,
And through the rugged path
Of life will lead thee sure.

Thy own life bury too
In other's hearts, I pray!
Then thou wilt live, though called
From earth by death, for aye.

CARL SIEBEL.

Mein Herz, ich will dich fragen.

Mein Herz, ich will dich fragen,
    Was ist denn Liebe, sag'?
„Zwei Seelen und ein Gedanke,
Zwei Herzen und ein Schlag!"

Und sprich, woher kommt Liebe?
„Sie kömmt und sie ist da!"
Und sprich, wie schwindet Liebe?
„Die war's nicht, der's geschah!"

Und was ist reine Liebe?
„Die ihrer selbst vergißt!"
Und wann ist Lieb' am tiefsten?
„Wenn sie am stillsten ist!"

LOVE.

My heart, what meaneth love,
    So speak, can'st tell me aught?
" Two hearts that beat as one,
Two souls, a single thought ! "

And speak, whence cometh love ?
" It cometh and is here."
How disappeareth love ?
" It cannot disappear."

And what is *pure* love ? " That
Which *self* forgetteth." When
Is love the deepest, pray ?
" When 'tis most silent, *then*."

Und wann ist Lieb' am reichsten?

„Das ist sie, wenn sie gibt!"

Und sprich, wie redet Liebe?

„Sie redet nicht, sie liebt!"

Friedrich Halm.

And when is love most rich?

"When it doth give." Doth e'er

Love speak, my truthful heart?

"It *loves*, it speaketh ne'er."

FRIEDRICH HALM.

Ich wollt' ein Sträußlein binden.

Ich wollt' ein Sträußlein binden,
    Da kam die dunkle Nacht,
Kein Blümlein war zu finden,
Sonst hätt' ich dir's gebracht.

Da flossen von den Wangen
Mir Thränen in den Klee,
Ein Blümlein aufgegangen
Ich nun im Garten seh'.

Das wollte ich dir brechen
Wohl in dem dunklen Klee,
Doch fing' es an zu sprechen:
„Ach, thue mir nicht weh!

I FAIN WOULD MAKE A NOSEGAY SWEET.

FAIN would make a nosegay sweet,
But night spread over me ;
Nowhere a flower my eye would meet,
Else I had brought it thee.

And down my cheeks did trickle tears
Into the grass,—and Oh !
A flower now so bright appears,
Where nothing then did grow.

I thought to pluck the flow'ret, dear,
There in the grassy plot,
But list, it speaketh, struck by fear :
" I pray thee hurt me not.

Sei freundlich in dem Herzen,

Betracht' dein eigen Leid,

Und laſſe mich in Schmerzen

Nicht ſterben vor der Zeit!"

Und hätt's nicht ſo geſprochen,

Im Garten ganz allein,

So hätt' ich dir's gebrochen,

Nun aber darf's nicht ſein.

Mein Schatz iſt ausgeblieben,

Ich bin ſo ganz allein,

Im Lieben wohnt Betrüben,

Und kann nicht anders ſein.

Clemens Brentano.

" Oh, in thy heart, pray, friendly be,

Of thy own sorrow think;

Before my time, do not let me

In death so painful sink."

Had it not thus appealed so sad,

So lovely and so fair,

I'd brought it thee, how glad, how glad;

But now I would not dare.

He comes not, *he* I love so well,

To dry the tears for me :

IN LOVE DOTH GRIEF AND SORROW DWELL,

AND THUS 'TWILL EVER BE.

CLEMENS BRENTANO.

Mutterherz.

Ich höre trauern euch und klagen,
    Daß kalt die Welt und liebeleer,
Und mitleidsvoll muß ich euch fragen:
Habt ihr denn keine Mutter mehr?

Habt ihr die Mutter schon vergessen,
Das treue Herz, d'ran ihr geruht,
Den Schooß, d'rin ihr so weich gesessen,
So sicher, wie in Gottes Hut?

Die Mutter fehlt mit süßen Schauern,
Die auf dem Arm ihr Kindlein trägt:
So lange wird die Liebe dauern,
So lang' ein Mutterherz noch schlägt!

MOTHER-HEART.

HEAR thee grieve so bitterly
That cold the world and loveless too;
And I must ask in sympathy,
Hast thou no more a mother true?

Forgotten hast the mother thine,
The heart on which wert wont to lie,
The lap on which didst warm recline,
Safe under God's all-seeing eye?

Contented rests the mother's eye,
While clasping close her babe so sweet;
Earth's loftiest love can never die
So long a mother's heart doth beat!

O Mutterherz, du Born der Milde,

Du gottgeweihter, heil'ger Ort,

Haßt auch die Welt, die rauhe, wilde,

In dir weilt still die Liebe fort!

Du lebst nur in des Kindes Leben,

Sonnst dich in seiner Freuden Glanz,

Sein Leiden nur macht dich erbeben,

Und deiner selbst vergißt du ganz.

Gequält, gemartet und zerstochen,

Liebst du im herbsten Schmerze noch,

Vom Kinde frevelnd selbst gebrochen,

Im Brechen segnest du es doch!

Oh ! mother-heart, thou holy source

Of love, thou consecrated spot,

Hates e'en the world, the rough, the coarse,

Thy quiet love is shaken not.

Thou livest for thy child alone,

Thou baskest in his pleasures sheen ;

His suff'rings only dost bemoan,

And thou thyself forgettest e'en.

Should he neglect thee, or forsake,

Though deep the wound, wouldst love not
    less ;

Were trifling he thy heart to break,

Him even then wouldst fondly bless.

D'rum, hält euch Gram und Leid umfangen,

Seid eigner Schuld ihr euch bewußt,

So lehnt die thränenfeuchten Wangen

An eurer Mutter treue Brust.

Und ist die Mutter euch geschieden,

Weint ihr allein in finstrer Nacht,

O glaubt: ihr Herz ließ sie hienieden,

Es hält bei ihrem Kinde wacht!

Albert Träger.

If sorrow thee as victim seeks,

Though thou hast played the baser part,

Go, place thy pale and tearful cheeks

Upon thy mother's loving heart.

Although thy mother dead may be,

If in the stilly night thou weep,

Believe, her heart brings her to thee,

It o'er her boy a watch doth keep !

ALBERT TRAEGER.

Der Wandrer geht alleine.

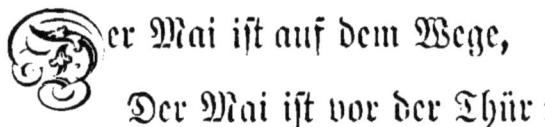

Der Mai ist auf dem Wege,
Der Mai ist vor der Thür:
Im Garten auf der Wiese,
Ihr Blümlein, kommt herfür!

Da hab' ich den Stab genommen,
Da hab' ich das Bündel geschnürt,
Zieh' weiter und immer weiter,
Wohin die Straße mich führt.

Und über mir ziehen die Vögel,
Sie ziehen in lustigen Reih'n;
Sie zwitschern und trillern und flöten,
Als ging's in den Himmel hinein.

THE WANDERER GOES ALONE.

Now May is on the road,
  Yes, May, sweet May is here;
In the garden, in the field,
Ye flowers, all appear.

I grasp my trusty staff
And strap my bundle tight,
And through the town I stride,
With heart and footstep light.

And o'er my head the birds
In merry flocks do fly;
Warbling and trilling, they
Do soar to Heaven high.

Der Wandrer geht alleine,

Geht schweigend seinen Gang;

Das Bündel will ihn drücken,

Der Weg wird ihm zu lang.

Ja, wenn wir allzusammen

So zögen in's Land hinein!

Und wenn auch das nicht wäre,

Könnt' Eine nur mit mir sein!

Wilhelm Müller.

The wand'rer goes alone,

He chants no merry song,

The bundle presses him,

The way it is so long.

Ah, could together we

All wander through the land !

Were this not, could but *she*

With me walk hand in hand !

WILHELM MUELLER.

Frühlingsgrüße.

Nach langem Frost, wie weht die
    Luft so lind!
Da bringt Frühveilchen mir ein bettelnd
    Kind.

Es ist betrübt, daß so den ersten Gruß

Des Frühlings mir das Elend bringen
    muß.

Und doch der schönen Tage liebes Pfand

Ist mir noch werther aus des Unglücks
    Hand.

So bringt dem Nachgeschlechte unser
    Leid
Die Frühlingsgrüße einer bessern Zeit.

Lenau.

SPRING'S GREETINGS.

THE zephyrs after lengthy frost,
    how mild!
Lo, violets fresh brings me a begging
    child.

'Tis sad, that thus Spring's greetings
    first should be
Presented me by hand of poverty,

And yet, the pledge of happy days
    the more
I prize, since offered by affliction sore.

Thus to posterity our ills do bring,

Foreboding better times, the hope of
    Spring.

LENAU.

Das Kind.

Ich schau' dich an wehmüthig
  Du blondgelocktes Kind,
Und fühl es tief, wie selig
Wohl deine Eltern sind.

Was ist das Gold der Reichen,
Was auf der Stirn ein Kranz,
Kind! gegen deine Locken
Und deiner Augen Glanz?

Und was sind alle Stimmen,
Vereint zu Ruhm und Preis,
Gegen dein süßes Lallen
Und——meine Thräne heiß?

THE CHILD.

SWEET child with golden ringlets,
Through tears I gaze on thee,
And deeply feel how happy
Thy parents ought to be.

What were the wealth of Crœsus,
The laurel wreath, my child,
To *thy* soft waving ringlets,
Thy glances tender, mild?

And what were all the voices
United to praise the great,
To *thy* sweet, artless prattling,
And these my tears of Fate?

O Kind! mir sagt dein Lallen:

Hast Lieb' und Lenz versäumt,

Und hast dein Leben einsam

In Liedern hingeträumt.

Adelheid Freiin von Stolterfoth.

My child, thy lispings tell me,

Neglecting Love and May,

Lonesome thou hast been dreaming

Thy life in songs away.

ADELHEID BARONESS VON STOLTERFOTH.

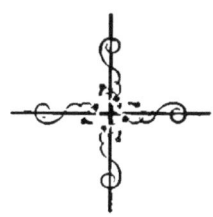

Nebel.

Du trüber Nebel, hülleft mir
Das Thal mit seinem Fluß,
Den Berg mit seinem Waldrevier
Und jeden Sonnengruß.

Nimm fort in deine graue Nacht
Die Erde weit und breit!
Nimm fort, was mich so traurig macht,
Auch die Vergangenheit!

Lenau.

THE FOG.

Thou dreary fog, for me dost vail
　　The forest and the stream,
The mountain and the lovely vale,
And every sunny beam.

Take then, Oh! take into thy night,
The wide, wide world, I pray;
What makes me sad, shut from my sight,
Take all the past away!

LENAU.

(Aus: Reiseblätter.)

Wanderung im Gebirge.

—

Erinnerung.

Du warst mir ein gar trauter, lieber
Geselle, komm, du schöner Tag,
Zieh noch einmal an mir vorüber,
Daß ich mich deiner freuen mag !

[From Leaves of Travel.]

WANDERING AMONG THE MOUNTAINS.

REMEMBRANCE.

THOU wast a trusty mate, wast dear

    To me, Oh, come thou happy day,

Before me do once more appear,

That I enjoy thy presence may.

Aufbruch.

Des Himmels frohes Antlitz brannte

Schon von des Tages erstem Kuß,

Und durch das Morgensternlein sandte

Die Nacht mir ihren Scheidegruß:

Da griff ich nach dem Wanderstabe,

Sprach meinem Wirthe: „Gott vergelt

Die Ruhestatt, die milde Labe!"

Zog lustig weiter in die Welt.

DEPARTURE.

THE face of Heaven glowed so
    bright
Kissed by the breaking morn, and
    through
The little morning star, the night
Did send to me its last adieu ;

Then I in hand my staff did take,
My host I thanked for all he'd done
My stay a pleasant one to make,
And light of heart, I journeyed on.

Die Lerche.

Froh summte nach der süßen Beute

Die Biene hin am Wiesensteg;

Die Lerche aus den Lüften streute

Mir ihre Lieder auf den Weg.

THE LARK.

So gaily hummed the busy bee

 For its sweet prize the mead along ;

The lark from Heaven's canopy

Did strew my path with merry song.

Der Eichwald.

Ich trat in einen heilig düstern
    Eichwald, da hört' ich leis' und lind
Ein Bächlein unter Blumen flüstern,
Wie das Gebet von einem Kind;

Und mich ergriff ein süßes Grauen,
Es rauscht' der Wald geheimnißvoll,
Als möcht' er mir was anvertrauen,
Das noch mein Herz nicht wissen soll;

Als möcht' er heimlich mir entdecken,
Was Gottes Liebe sinnt und will:
Doch schien er plötzlich zu erschrecken
Vor Gottes Näh'—und wurde still.

THE FOREST OF OAKS.

A FOREST dark of sacred oak
  I entered, where soft and mild
'Neath flowers fair, a brooklet spoke—
'Twas like the prayer of a child.

With strange delight awe thrilled my
    heart,
The forest rang mysteriously,
As if it something would impart
That ought not yet be told to me.

As if the secret 'twould reveal,
What God's great love doth plan and will,
But suddenly it seemed to feel
His presence near—and all was still.

Der Hirte.

Schon zog vom Wald ich ferne wieder
    Auf einer steilen Alpenwand;
Doch blickt ich oft zu ihm hinnieder,
Bis mir sein letzter Wipfel schwand.

Da irrten Küh' am Wiesenhange;
Der Hirte unterm Kieferdach
Hing still bei ihrem Glockenklange
Dem Bilde seines Liebchens nach.

THE SHEPHERD.

FROM the forest I did farther go,

On alpine rocks of dizzy height;

But often at the trees below

I gazed, till all were lost to sight.

The herds upon the mead I saw;

The shepherd, by the music of

Their bells, beneath his cot of straw,

Mused o'er the image of his Love.

Einsamkeit.

Schon seh' ich Hirt' und Heerde nimmer,

Ein Lüftchen nur ist mein Geleit;

Der steile Pfad wird steiler immer,

Es wächst die wilde Einsamkeit.

Dort stürzt aus dunkler Felsenpforte

Der Quell mit einem bangen Schrei,

Enteilt dem grauenvollen Orte,

Hinab zum freundlich grünen Mai.

Verschwunden ist das letzte Leben,

Hier grünt kein Blatt, kein Vogel ruft,

Und selbst der Pfad scheint hier zu beben,

So zwischen Wand und Todeskluft.

SOLITUDE.

Now shepherd, herds—I see them
        never,
My only guide's a zephyr kind;

The path so steep, grows steeper ever,

'Mid solitude myself I find.

From sombre rocks a streamlet clear,

With timid cry, doth quickly bound,

It flees the spot, so sterile, drear,

Down where sweet May adorns the
        ground.

No sign of life around is seen,

No leaflet greens,* no birdling calls,

To quake doth seem the pathway e'en,

'Tween Death's abyss and towering
        walls.

*Greened all the year.—THOMSON.

Komm, Gottesläugner, Gott zu fühlen;

Dein Frevel wird auf diesem Rand

Den Todesabgrund tiefer wühlen,

Dir steiler thürmen diese Wand!—

Come, disbeliever, feel God's power!

While struck with awe thou hold'st thy
    breath;
Before thy eyes these walls will tower

Still higher on the brink of Death!

Die Ferne.

Des Berges Gipfel war erschwungen,

    Der trotzig in die Tiefe schaut;

Natur, von deinem Reiz durchdrungen,

    Wie schlug mein Herz so frei so laut!

Behaglich streckte dort das Land sich

In Ebnen aus, weit, endlos weit,

Mit Thürmen, Wald und Flur, und wand sich

Der Ströme Zier um's bunte Kleid;

Hier stieg es plötzlich und entschlossen

Empor, stets kühner himmelan,

Mit Eis und Schnee das Haupt umgossen,

Vertrat den Wolken ihre Bahn.

THE DISTANCE.

THE peak was gained, 'twas hard
    to climb,
Downward it frowned defiantly ;

Thrilled Nature with thy charms
    sublime,
My heart did throb so loud and free !

An endless plain did meet my view,

With steeples, forests, pretty farms,

Its dress of variegated hue

Was trimmed with many a river's
    charms.

Here loomed it upward in a trice,

Up, up to Heaven's starlit vault,

Its brow, bedecked with snow and ice,

E'en bade the flying clouds to halt.

Bald hing mein Auge freudetrunken

Hier an den Felsen, schroff und wild;

Bald war die Seele still versunken

Dort in der Ferne Räthselbild.

Die dunkle Ferne sandte leise

Die Sehnsucht, ihre Schwester, mir,

Und rasch verfolgt' ich meine Reise

Den Berg hinab, zu ihr, zu ihr:

Wie manchen Zauber mag es geben,

Den die Natur auch dort ersann;

Wie mancher Biedre mag dort leben,

Dem ich die Hand noch drücken kann!

Spellbound I viewed the mountain's
   crest,
Its rugged sides, its aspect wild,

Abstracted then my eye would rest,

Upon the distant picture mild.

The sombre distance still did send

To me its kindred, longing sweet,

And down the slope I then did wend

My way, its mysteries to meet.

There may be many a magic spell

By Nature wrought in yonder land;

There many an honest man may dwell,

Whom I could give my heart and
   hand.

Das Gewitter.

Doch immer lag ein tiefes Schweigen
    Rings auf den Höh'n; doch
        plötzlich fuhr
Der Wind nun auf zum wilden Reigen,
Die sausende Gewitterspur.

Am Himmel eilt mit dumpfem Klange
Herauf der finstre Wolkenzug:
So nimmt der Zorn im heißen Drange
Den nächtlichen Gedankenflug.

Der Himmel donnert seinen Hader;
Auf seiner dunkeln Stirne glüht
Der Blitz hervor, die Zornesader,
Die Schrecken auf die Erde sprüht.

THE STORM.

A n om'nous silence still doth reign
 Upon the heights, when suddenly
The wind doth blow a hurricane,—
Foretelling that a storm is nigh.

Upward the clouds advance in force,
With sounds so dull and black as night;
Thus anger in its fiery course
Doth take thought's melancholy flight.

Heav'n's thunder roareth, crash on crash;
Upon its threat'ning brow doth glow
Dread anger's vein, the lightning's flash,
And terror spreads on earth below.

Der Regen stürzt in lauten Güssen;

Mit Bäumen, die der Sturm zerbrach,

Erbraust der Strom zu meinen Füßen;—

Doch schweigt der Donner allgemach.

Der Sturm läßt seine Flügel sinken,

Der Regen säuselt milde Ruh;

Da sah ich froh ein Hüttlein winken

Und eilte seiner Pforte zu.

In torrents loud the rain doth gush,

And at my feet the stream, with trees

Uprooted by the storm, doth rush ;—

The thunder dieth by degrees.

The storm, aweary, sinks to sleep,

And mild repose bespeaks the rain—

I see a cot thro' foliage peep,

And speed its shelter to obtain.

Der Schlaf.

Ein Greis trat lächelnd mir entgegen,
  Bot mir die Hand gedankenvoll,
Und hob sie dann empor zum Segen,
Der sanft vom Himmel niederquoll;

Und ich empfand es tief im Herzen,
Daß Zorn der Donner Gottes nicht;
Daß aus der Weste leichten Scherzen
Wie aus Gewittern Liebe spricht.

Und einen Labebecher trank ich,
Und schlich, wohin die Ruh mich rief,
Hinaus zur Scheune; müde sank ich
Hier in des Heues Duft—und schlief.

SLEEP.

 GRAY haired man here met my eye;

He smiled, gave me his hand, and
— lo!
Then for a blessing raised it high,

That softly from above did flow.

I deeply felt it in my breast,

That not God's wrath doth thunder tell,

That in the zephyrs of the west,

Like in the tempests Love doth dwell.

A cooling cup I gladly drank,

In search of rest then eager stepped

Out to the barn, and weary sank

Upon the fragrant hay and—slept.

Was mich erfreut auf meinen Wegen,

Das träumt' ich nun im Schlafe nach;

Und träumend hört' ich, wie der Regen

Sanft niederträufelt' auf das Dach.

Süß träumt es sich in einer Scheune,

Wenn drauf der Regen leise klopft;

So mag sich's ruhn im Todtenschreine,

Auf den die Freundeszähre tropft.

What on the way my heart did cheer,

I in my sleep dreamt over again,

And dreaming, I did lightly hear

Upon the roof the pattering rain.

One in a barn can dream with zest,

When on it taps the rain above;

Thus in the coffin we may rest,

When on it falls the tear of Love.

Der Abend.

Die Wolken waren fortgezogen,
Die Sonne strahlt' im Untergang,
Und am Gebirg der Regenbogen,
Als ich von meinem Lager sprang.

Da griff ich nach dem Wanderstabe,
Sprach meinem Wirth ein herzlich Wort
Für Ruhestatt und milde Labe,
Und zog in stiller Dämmrung fort.

Lenau.

THE sky was blue, the clouds had gone,

The setting sun bright rays did shed,

And on the mount the rainbow shone,

When I refreshed did leave my bed.

I grasped my staff, kind friend to me,

And for my short, but pleasant stay,

I thanked my host right heartily ;

In twilight still then went my way.

LENAU.

Lenz.

Die Bäume blühn,
   Die Vöglein singen,
Die Wiesen bringen
Ihr erstes Grün.

Schier thut's mir leid,
Zu treten die Erden
Und ihr zu gefährden
Ihr neues Kleid.

Sie hat nicht Acht,
Ob Knospenspringen
Und Frühlingssingen
Mich traurig macht.

Lenau.

SPRING.

Now buds are seen,
　　The birds are singing,
The meads are bringing
Their virgin green.

I feel distress
The earth to trample,
To spoil her ample,
Her pretty dress.

But what cares she
If flowers springing,
And vernal singing,
Give pain to me.

LENAU.

Wanderlied.

Wohlauf! noch getrunken
　Den funkelnden Wein!
Ade nun, ihr Lieben!
Geschieden muß sein.
Ade nun, ihr Berge,
Du väterlich Haus!
Es treibt in die Ferne
Mich mächtig hinaus.

Die Sonne, sie bleibet
Am Himmel nicht stehn,
Es treibt sie, durch Länder
Und Meere zu gehn.
Die Woge nicht haftet
Am einsamen Strand,
Die Stürme, sie brausen
Mit Macht durch das Land.

WANDER SONG.

CHEER up, let us drink yet
   The wine sparkling, clear !
Farewell, I must part now
From all that is dear !
Farewell ye old hill tops,
Dear birth place, my home !
Out in the wide world, I
Am goaded to roam !

On the blue arch of Heaven
The sun will not stay,
O'er land it is driven
And sea far away.
The waves they while never
At the lonely strand,
The storms do rush ever
With might through the land.

Mit eilenden Wolken
Der Vogel doch zieht,
Und singt in der Ferne
Ein heimathlich Lied.
So treibt es den Burschen
Durch Wälder und Feld,
Zu gleichen der Mutter,
Der wandernden Welt.

Da grüßen ihn Vögel
Bekannt über'm Meer,
Sie flogen von Fluren
Der Heimath hieher,
Da duften die Blumen
Vertraulich um ihn,
Sie trieben vom Lande
Die Lüfte dahin.

With the clouds on high flying
The birdlings do roam,
And sing, far away, a
Song of sweet home.
The youth through the forest
Is driven, o'er lea,
Like the mother world, he
Too roveth free.

Here birdlings do greet him,
To him so well known,
From the garden of home, they
Have after him flown.
Here flowers most fair, all
Around him he finds,
From home, their sweet fragrance
Was borne by the winds.

Die Vögel, die kennen

Sein väterlich Haus.

Die Blumen einst pflanzt' er

Der Liebe zum Strauß,

Und Liebe, die folgt ihm,

Sie geht ihm zur Hand:

So wird ihm zur Heimath

Das fernefte Land.

Justinus Kerner.

The abode of his father

The birdlings well knew,

The flowers *he* raised, for

His maiden they grew.

And Love him escorteth,

His true guiding star:

Thus home the youth findeth

In country afar.

JUSTINUS KERNER.

Rückblick.

Da lieg' ich still und traure,
    Mein Herz ist von Weh erfüllt,
Voll Sehnsucht denk' ich wieder
An ein entschwund'nes Bild.

O wärst du mir geblieben,
Ein Engel zur Seite mir,
Ich wäre nimmer geworden
Der düstere Fremdling hier.

Ich hätte mein Herz bewahret
Vor mancher wilden That;
Ich wäre so rein geblieben,
So rein ich dir genaht.

Christian Döppl.

RETROSPECTION.

'M lying still, and mourning,
For gone's life's brightest ray;
And anxiously I'm dreaming
Of an image passed away.

Hadst thou remained an angel
To me, forever near,
Become, I should have, never,
The gloomy stranger here.

My heart I should have guarded
'Gainst many an action free;
Remained so pure and loving,
And thought of naught but thee.

CHRISTIAN HOEPPL.

Die Drei.

Drei Reiter, nach verlorner Schlacht,
Wie reiten sie so sacht, so sacht!

Aus tiefen Wunden quillt das Blut,
Es spürt das Roß die warme Flut.

Vom Sattel tropft das Blut, vom Zaum,
Und spült hinunter Staub und Schaum.

Die Rosse schreiten sanft und weich,
Sonst flöß' das Blut zu rasch, zu reich.

Die Reiter reiten dicht gesellt,
Und einer sich am andern hält.

THE THREE.

THREE riders after sore defeat
    From battle-field so still retreat!

From ghastly wounds doth course
    their blood,
The horses feel Life's ebbing flood.

The blood drips, drips from man and horse,

Takes dust and froth down in its course.

The horses pace so very slow,

Else would the gore too quickly flow.

The horsemen sway from side to side,

And not to fall, do closely ride.

Sie sehn sich traurig in's Gesicht,

Und einer um den andern spricht:

„Mir blüht daheim die schönste Maid,

Drum thut mein früher Tod mir leid,"

„Hab' Haus und Hof und grünen Wald,

Und sterben hier muß ich so bald!"

„Den Blick hab' ich in Gottes Welt,

Sonst nichts, doch schwer mir's Sterben
    fällt."

Und lauernd auf den Todesritt

Ziehn durch die Luft drei Geier mit.

Sie theilen kreischend unter sich:

„Den speisest du, den du, den ich."

Lenau.

Sad they at one another gaze,
What most he feels thus each one
   says :

" At home a maid for me doth sigh,
Therefore I dread so soon to die ! "

" Have garden, house and greenwood
   dear,
And doomed to die so soon I'm
   here!"

"In God's wide world the view have I,
Naught more, yet 'tis so hard to die!"

The ride of death three birds of prey
Do watch and follow all the way.

Thus they divide and harshly cry :
" Him eatest thou, him thou, him I ! "

LENAU.

Heimath.

Und ich liebe sie doch! — — —
   Dumpf und trübe
Nannte ich oft
Die Glocken der Heimath,
Doch heut' klingen sie über das Meer
So wehmuthselig,
So wunderbarlich,
Daß selbst mein lachendes Herz
Ihr Echo wird.

Wie ein Bild der Zauberin,
Der Dichterfreundin Morgana,
Erblick' ich fern am Horizonte
Wehmüthig winkend
Die Gärten und Wiesen,

HOME.

 ND I love it still!

Dull and mournful

Often I called

The bells of my home ; but

To day over the Ocean they sound

So sadly blissful,

So strange and doleful,

That even my laughing heart

Their echo becomes.

Like a picture of the sorceress,

The poet's friend Morgana,

I see afar on the horizon,

Beckoning sadly,

The gardens and meadows,

Das schwarzbeschieferte Haus

Mit den grünen Fenstern,

Und am Fenster zum Garten

Seh' ich die Mutter.

Auf ihren Knieen

Ruhet ein Buch—

Sie liest in dem Buche.

Ich seh' es genau,

Es ist das Buch,

Das einst dem Sohne

Mit Thränen sie schenkte,

Und das der Sohn,

Als er fortging,

Vergaß.

The old black slated house
With its windows green, and
At the garden side window,
I see my mother.

Upon her knees, there,
Resteth a book,
She readeth therein.
I plainly can see
It is the same book
She once presented,
With tears, to her son,
And which her son,
When he left her,
Forgot.

Sie liest die Worte,

Die eigenhändig

Aus warmem Herzen „zu stetem Gedenken"

Sie eingeschrieben—

Ich glaub', eine Thräne

Fällt heiß auf die Bibil.—

Wehmüthig über das Meer

Klingen die Glocken der Heimath.

Carl Siebel.

She reads the words, that

She with her own hands,

With overflowing heart, "for constant
remembrance,"
Therein did inscribe.

A tear methinketh,

Falls hot on the Bible.

Woefully over the sea

Sound the bells of sweet home.

CARL SIEBEL.

Lebewohl.

Wer sollte fragen: wie's geschah?
Es geht auch Andern eben so.
Ich freute mich, als ich dich sah,
Du warst, als du mich sahst, auch froh.

Der erste Gruß, den ich dir bot,
Macht' uns auf einmal beide reich;
Du wurdest, als ich kam, so roth,
Du wurdest, als ich ging, so bleich.

Nun kam ich auch Tag aus, Tag ein,
Es ging uns beiden durch den Sinn;
Bei Regen und bei Sonnenschein
Schwand bald der Sommer uns dahin.

FAREWELL.

WHO should inquire : " How was it,
    pray ? "
It happens oft to others too :

I gazed on you, Love shed his ray,

You gazed on me and lived anew.

The first " good morrow " that I said,

Struck chords of love, this both did
    know,
For when I came, you turned so red,

And turned so pale, when I did go.

And soon I came day after day ;

Ours was indeed a happy lot ;

'Mid sunshine, rain, soon passed away

Sweet Summer, rose, forget me not.

Wir haben uns die Hand gedrückt,

Um nichts gelacht, um nichts geweint,

Gequält einander und beglückt,

Und haben's redlich auch gemeint.

Dann kam der Herbst, der Winter gar,

Die Schwalbe zog, nach altem Brauch,

Und: lieben?—lieben immerdar?

Es wurde kalt, es fror uns auch.

Ich werde geh'n in's fremde Land,

Du sagst mir höflich: Lebe wohl!

Ich küße höflich dir die Hand,

Und nun ist alles wie es soll.

Adelbert von Chamisso.

We did what e'er dictated Love :

We cared for naught, we shed no tear,

Our love like that of turtle dove

I thought, it seemed so pure, sincere.*

Leaves fell, soon snow was at our door,

To warmer climes the swallows flew,

And love? what, love forevermore?

It grew so cold, we felt it too.

I leave now for a foreign land,

You coldly say, " farewell," to me,

Politely I do kiss thy hand,—

And all things are as they should be.

ADELBERT VON CHAMISSO.

---

* This stanza is paraphrastical.

Der Kranke im Garten.

Noch eine Nachtigall, so spät?
    Schon sind die Blüthen
      längst verweht,
Der Sommer reift die Felder schon,

Und noch ein Frühlingston?

O Lenz, ward es dir offenbar,

Daß ich noch sterbe dieses Jahr?

Und riefest aus der Ferne du

Noch einen Gruß mir zu?—

Lenau.

THE INVALID IN THE GARDEN.

NIGHTINGALE so late yet? Oh !

The blossoms fell, ay, long ago,

Now ripe the fields from summerheat,

And still a song of Spring so sweet?

Ah, Spring, was it revealed that I

Must part from all this year, must die?

And from afar, didst kindly send

To me a greeting yet, dear friend?

LENAU.

Heimkehr.

In meine Heimath kam ich wieder,
Es war die alte Heimath noch,
Dieselbe Luft, dieselben Lieder,
Und Alles war ein Andres doch.

Die Welle rauschte wie vor Zeiten,
Am Waldweg sprang wie sonst das Reh,
Von fern erklang ein Abendläuten,
Die Berge glänzten aus dem See.

Doch vor dem Haus, wo uns vor Jahren
Die Mutter stets empfing, dort sah
Ich fremde Menschen fremd gebahren;
Wie weh, wie weh mir da geschah!

RETURN-HOME.

HOME I returned, had wandered long,
'Twas still the home that I had left;
The same sweet air, the merry song,
And yet it was of all bereft!

The wavelets rippled as of yore,
Across the sward did bound the stag,
The bells were chiming as before,
The lake reflected mount and crag.

But at the house where years ago
Mother received me kindly oft,
Strangers were walking to and fro;
I raised my hands to Him aloft!

Mir war, als rief' es aus den Wogen:

Flieh, flieh, und ohne Wiederkehr!

Die du geliebt, sind fortgezogen,

Sie kehren nimmer, nimmermehr.

Hermann Lingg.

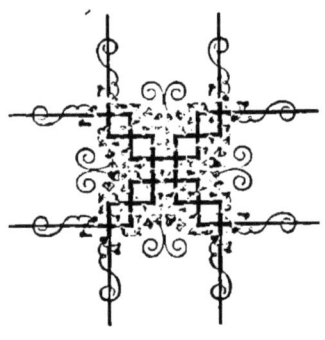

Methought a voice in the wavelets near

Cried: " Fly, Oh fly, and leave this shore !

Those whom you loved, have gone from
here,

Return they'll never, never more !"

HERMANN LINGG.

Der Weg zum Paradiese.

Was will das Kind nur wieder
 Am Spittel vor dem Thor,
Was pocht es doch nur immer
Und wimmert so davor?

„Ich suche meine Mutter,
Ach, laßt zu ihr mich ein!
Sie trugen vor zwei Monden
Zu euch sie ja hinein.“

„Du armes, armes Mädchen,
Du dauerst mich wohl sehr,
Doch deine Mutter findest
Du nun und nimmermehr.

THE WAY TO PARADISE.

WHAT wilt again thou, maiden,
   Here at the hospital door?
Why art forever tapping
And wailing, speak, wherefore?

"I'm here to seek my mother;
Oh, let me enter, pray!
Here two months since they brought her,
Full well I know the day!"

"Poor child, Oh! I do deeply
Thy bitter lot deplore;
Thou'lt find thy own dear mother,
Here never, nevermore.

Die liegt seit sieben Tagen

Bereits im kühlen Grund."

So spricht der alte Pförtner

Und schließt das Thor zur Stund'.

Wohl steht da vor dem Spittel

Das Kind und weint und klagt,

Denn nimmer hat's verstanden,

Was Jener ihm gesagt.

Dann schleicht es still und trauernd

Zurück, woher es kam,

Zur Alten, die es pfleget,

Seit Gott die Mutter nahm.

" For in her gràve she slumbers ;

'Tis now the seventh day ! "

Thus speaks the hoary keeper,

Then sadly turns away.

And at the gate the maiden

Wailing and weeping staid,

Far naught she comprehendeth

What he to her hath said.

Then sorrowful she wendeth

Her way, from whence she came,

To her who gave her shelter,

A kind and goodly dame.

Doch schon am Morgen wieder

Steht's vor dem Spittel dort

Und pocht sich wund die Händchen

Und will vom Thor nicht fort.

„O Pförtner, schlimmer Pförtner,

O laß zum Thor mich ein!

Kann ja daheim nicht bleiben,

Wenn fort das Mütterlein."

„Dein Mütterlein, du Aermste,

Für immer dich verließ,

Denn wiss' es nur, sie wohnet

Ja jetzt im Paradies."

But at the dawn of morning

Again she tries the door,

And will not leave, but tappeth

E'en till her hands grow sore.

"Oh, keeper, cruel keeper,

Do let me enter, pray !

At home I cannot linger

When mother is away."

"Thou hapless child, thy mother

Hath left forever thee ;

In Paradise she dwelleth,

From earthly sorrows free !"

D'rauf schließt das Thor sich wieder;

Da steht allein das Kind

Und sinnt, wie's nur die Straße

Zum Paradiese sind'.

Und fort mit nacktem Füßchen,

Im Röckchen dünn und leicht,

Geht's dann auf stein'gem Pfade,

Das Aug' von Thränen feucht.

Und freundlich fragt es Jeden,

Der seinem Weg sich naht:

„Wo ist zum Paradiese,

O sagt, der rechte Pfad?"

The gate again he locketh;

Alone the maid doth stay,

And ponder to discover

To Paradise the way.

Barefooted then she wanders

On, over hill and dale,

However rough the pathway,

And looks so sad and pale.

And every one that meets her,

She asks with tearful eyes:

"Show me the way that leadeth,

I pray, to Paradise!"

Doch Jeder spricht: „Ho, Kindchen,

Dein Weg ist rauh und weit!

Geb' Gott in seiner Milde

Dahin dir das Geleit!"

Doch kann auch Keiner künden

Ihm, wo der theure Ort,

So geht doch unaufhaltsam

Das Mägdlein fort und fort.

Schon sinkt mit ihren Schauern

Herab die finst're Nacht,

Da faltet fromm die Händchen

Das Kind und betet sacht.

But every one says: " Maiden,

The way is long and wide !

May God in tender mercy,

Thy leader be and guide ! "

Yet no one can inform her

Where lies the treasured spot,

So she doth wander, wander

On, falt'ring, ling'ring not.

The shades of night are falling,

Ere she, too weary, stays ;

Then piously she foldeth

Her little hands and prays.

Dann hinter gold'nen Garben

Puppt sich die Kleine ein,

Bis wundermild umschimmert

Das Feld der Sonne Schein.

Und wieder geht sie weiter

Und fleht: „O saget an,

Wo ich zum Paradiese

Den Weg nur finden kann?

Da dauert wohl die Leute

Das Kind in seiner Noth,

Manch' eine fromme Mutter

Beschenkt's mit Obst und Brod.

Behind some golden sheaves then,

In slumber sinks the child,

Till o'er the field doth glimmer

The morning sun so mild.

Again she journeys farther,

Imploring : " Tell me, pray !

To Paradise how can I,

How can I find the way ? "

Hearts ache to see her carry

So young misfortune's load;

Good mothers fondly feed her

And cheer her on her road.

So wandert immer weiter
Von Ort zu Ort das Kind,
Schon sind ihm wund vom Gehen
Die Füßchen zart und lind.

Zerrauft sind seine Härchen,
Die Wänglein hohl und blaß,
Sein dünnes Röcklein träufelt,
Wie ist's vom Regen naß!

So sind an vierzehn Tage
Entfloh'n im Lauf der Zeit,
Seit fort das Kind gewandert
Vom Vaterhaus so weit.

Still wanders ever farther,

So helpless and alone,

From constant walking weary,

The motherless unknown.

Her tresses too are matted,

Her cheeks have lost their hue,

Her tattered gown is dripping,

So wet from rain and dew.

Thus fourteen days have vanished,

For time doth linger not,

Since forth the child did wander

From her paternal cot.

Und immer mehr entschwindet

Dem Aermsten Muth und Kraft,

Kaum kann sich's fort mehr schleppen

Auf seiner Pilgerschaft.

Doch sieh', da ragt ein Kloster

Zum Wolkenzelt hinauf,

Im Morgenschimmer flimmert

Der Thürme goldner Knauf.

Dahin schleppt sich die Kleine,

Dort sucht sie Rath und Trost,

Schon lehnt sie müd' am Thore

Und pocht, durchbebt von Frost.

She's now well nigh exhausted,

Is filled with blank despair,

The cross hath been too heavy

For the little one to bear.

Behold yon nunn'ry tow'ring

On high to the planets' home;

In the morning light doth glitter

The lofty, gilded dome.

Oh, thither she doth stagger,

There comfort she doth seek,

Against the door she leaneth

And tappeth, numbed and weak.

Wohl tritt da eine Nonne

Heraus zum Thor geschwind :

„Was suchst du, so verlassen,

Bei uns, du armes Kind ? ”—

"Ich suche meine Mutter,

Die mich zum Leid verließ,

Und kann den Weg nicht finden

Zu ihr in's Paradies.”—

„Du arme, arme Waise ! ”

So seufzt die Gottesbraut,

Und führt hinein die Kleine,

Die fragend zu ihr schaut.

Thus summoned by the maiden,

A nun doth soon appear :

" What wilt thou, so forsaken,

With us my little dear ? "

"In Paradise my mother,

'Tis she whom long I've sought,

But of the way to find it

No one can tell me aught."

" Poor waif, so true and loving ! "

The bride of Heaven sighs,

And leads within the maiden,

Who stares with wond'ring eyes.

Doch ach, wie da nur rüttelt's

Mit Eins das Kind so wild!

Hin sinkt's, zum Tod ermattet,

Ein sterbend Engelsbild.

Wohl eilen all' die Schwestern

Voll haft'ger Sorg' herbei,

Geschäftig, fromm ihm bringend

Manch' kräft'ge Arzenei.

Und jede drängt mit Weinen

Sich zu dem Kindlein süß;

Doch schon hat dies gefunden

Den Weg zum Paradies.

Johann N. Vogl.

Alas! how now doth tremble

The little girl of care ;

She sinks, to death exhausted,

A dying angel fair.

Now all the sisters hasten

To the little one's relief,

Bring spirits to restore her,

And try to soothe her grief.

And they with deep emotion

Press 'round the child and pray ;

But she hath found, thank Heaven !

To Paradise the way.

JOHANN N. VOGL.

Trockne Blumen.

Ihr Blümlein alle,
    Die sie mir gab,
Euch soll man legen
Mit mir in's Grab.

Wie seht ihr alle
Mich an so weh,
Als ob ihr wüßtet,
Wie mir gescheh'?

Ihr Blümlein alle,
Wie welk, wie blaß!
Ihr Blümlein alle,
Wovon so naß?

WITHERED FLOWERS.

H, flow'rets all
   That she me gave,
Ye shall with me
Lie in my grave!

Ye look at me
So sad and true,
As if my woes
Full well ye knew!

Ye flow'rets all,
How withered, sere!
Whence then so wet,
My flow'rets dear?

Ach Thränen machen

Nicht maiengrün,

Machen todte Liebe

Nicht wieder blühn.

Und Lenz wird kommen,

Und Winter wird gehn,

Und Blümlein werden

Im Grase stehn,

Und Blümlein liegen

In meinem Grab,

Die Blümlein alle,

Die sie mir gab.

Oh! tears will make

No green of May,

Nor make dead love

See light of day.

Soon Spring will come,

And Winter pass,

And flow'rets bright

Will stud the grass.

And flow'rets will

Lie in my grave,

These flow'rets all

That she me gave.

Und wenn sie wandelt

Am Hügel vorbei,

Und denkt im Herzen:

Der meint' es treu!

Dann, Blümlein, alle

Heraus, heraus!

Der Mai ist kommen,

Der Winter ist aus.

Wilhelm Müller.

Should she the mound

Be passing near,   .

Think in her heart :

He was sincere—

Then flow'rets all

Burst forth and bloom!

Sweet May hath come,

Gone Winter's gloom.

WILHELM MUELLER.

Erheiterung durch Thränen.

Die Wolken ziehn herüber
So dicht gedrängt und grau,
Und trüber, immer trüber
Wird rings des Himmels Blau.

Und du, wie ist entflogen
Dir alle Heiterkeit,
Die Seele überzogen
Von unnennbarem Leid!

Die Wolken strömen nieder,
Wie blau der Himmel scheint!
Wie heiter bist du wieder!
Hast du vielleicht geweint?

C. J. Ph. Spitta.

CONSOLATION THROUGH TEARS.

DARK clouds are hurrying fast;
    The Heaven blue and bright
Is quickly overcast—
And day is turned to night.

From thee all joy and jest
Have taken wings and flown;
Within thy soul doth rest
Some silent grief unknown.

The clouds pour down in rain,
The Heaven blue appears,
How merry thou'rt again :
Hast thou been shedding tears ?

C. J. PHILIP SPITTA.

Nach Jahren.

I.

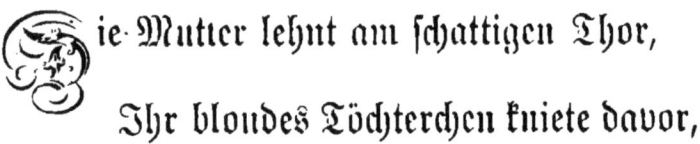

ie Mutter lehnt am schattigen Thor,

Ihr blondes Töchterchen kniete davor,

Brach Rosen sich und Vergißmeinnicht,

Und küßt sie mit lachendem Angesicht:

„Ei! Mutter, bin ich so groß wie du,

Dann trag' ich dir Alles im Hause zu,

Dann heg' ich und pfleg' ich dich lieb und fein,

Wie die Rosen und die Vergißnichtmein."

THE LAPSE OF YEARS.

I.

IN the doorway stands the mother mild,
  Before her kneels her darling child.

Plucks roses red, entwined with green
And kisses her with laughing mien :

" When I like thee have grown so tall,
Ask what thou wilt, I'll bring it all.

Will nurse and tend thee well and fine,
As now the rose and fragile vine ! "

II.

Und Jahre schwanden,—am schattigen Thor

Ragt höher und voller der Flieder empor!

Ein Mägdlein umfaßt des Geliebten Arm,

Es schlagen ihre Herzen so treu und warm;

Doch wie sie sich küßten auf Wang' und Mund,

Weinte das Mädchen aus Herzensgrund;

Denn die sie wollt' pflegen so lieb und fein,

Lag still unter Ros' und Vergißnichtmein.

Adolf Böttger.

II.

Years have elapsed,—around the door
The vines cling closer than of yore ;

A maid leans on her lover's arm,
Their hearts are beating true and warm.

As he imprints upon her brow
A burning kiss, she weeps ; for now

She whom she wished to tend so fine,
Lies cold 'neath rose and ivy vine.

ADOLF BŒTTGER.

An den Frühling.

Noch immer, Frühling, bist du nicht
Gekommen in mein Thal,
Wo ich dein liebes Angesicht
Begrüßt das letztemal.

Noch steh'n die Bäume dürr und baar
Um deinen Weg herum
Und strecken, eine Bettlerschaar,
Nach dir die Arme stumm.

Frühblumen wähnten dich schon hier,
Frost bringt sie um ihr Glück,
Sie sehnten sich heraus nach dir,
Und können nicht zurück.

TO SPRING.

THOU art not come yet, Spring so sweet,
  Into my valley, Oh,
Where I thy presence mild did greet,
With songs a year ago !

Along thy path the trees still stand,
So bare and cheerless, see !
They stretch their arms, a begging band,
In silent prayer to thee.

The early flowers thought wert here,
Frost turned their joy to pain :
They longed to be where *thou* wert near,—
Cannot return again.

Die Schwalbe fliegt bestürzt umher,
Und ruft nach dir voll Gram,
Bereut schon, daß sie über's Meer
Zu früh herüberkam.

Lenau.

The swallow flies like lost, in pain

It calleth after thee,

Regretting that it came again

Too soon across the sea.

LENAU.

Einst und Jetzt.

Möchte wieder in die Gegend,
     „Wo ich einst so selig war,
„Wo ich lebte, wo ich träumte
„Meiner Jugend schönstes Jahr!"

Also sehnt' ich in der Ferne
Nach der Heimath mich zurück,
Wähnend, in der alten Gegend
Finde sich das alte Glück.

Endlich ward mir nun beschieden,
Wiederkehr in's traute Thal;
Doch es ist dem Heimgekehrten
Nicht zu Muth wie dazumal.

ONCE AND NOW.

"OULD I once more see the country,
  Where I only knew of joy,
Where I dwelt and where I dreamt, a
Wayward, thoughtless, merry boy ! "

Thus my heart in foreign country
Longed for home, 'mong strangers cold,
Thinking in my native land, that
I would find the joys of old.

And at last it was decreed, that
I should see my home again,
But alas ! my heart's rejoicings
Sadly are alloyed with pain.

Wie man grüßet alte Freunde,

Grüß' ich manchen lieben Ort;

Doch im Herzen wird so schwer mir,

Denn mein Liebstes ist ja fort.

Immer schleicht sich noch der Pfad hin

Durch das dunkle Waldrevier;

Doch er führt die Mutter Abends

Nimmermehr entgegen mir.

Mögen deine Grüße rauschen

Vom Gestein, du trauter Bach;

Doch der Freund ist mir verloren,

Der in dein Gemurmel sprach.

As we greet old friends, I greet with

Warmth the haunts of old so dear,

But my heart is well nigh breaking,

For my Love hath gone from here.

Through the sombre forest traileth

Still the pathway as of yore,

But to me at eve it leadeth

Mother, never, nevermore.

Though thy greetings rustle mildly,

Lovely brook, from stone to stone,

Still the friend that in thy murm'rings

Spoke once, is forever gone.

Baum, wo sind die Nachtigallen,

Die hier sangen einst so süß?

Und wo, Wiese, deine Blumen,

Die mir Rosa sinnend wies?—

Blumen fort und Nachtigallen,

Und das gute Mädchen auch!

Meine Jugend fort mit ihnen;

Alles wie ein Frühlingshauch!

Lenau.

Tree, where are the nightingales, that

Sang so sweetly and so low,

And where, meadow, are the flowers,

Rose to me was wont to show?

Nightingales and flowers vanished,

And the maiden goodly, fair,

And my youthful dreams of pleasure,

Like a breath of vernal air.

LENAU.

Wohl heute noch und morgen—

Wo's schneiet rothe Rosen,
Da regnet's Thranen d'rein.

Wohl heute noch und morgen
    Da bleibe ich bei dir,
Wenn aber kommt der dritte Tag,
So muß ich fort von hier."

„Wann kommst du aber wieder,
Herzallerliebster mein,
Und brichst die rothen Rosen
Und trinkst den kühlen Wein?"

„Wenn's schneiet rothe Rosen,
Wenn's regnet kühlen Wein;
So lang' sollst du noch harren,
Herzallerliebste mein!"

TO-DAY YET AND TO-MORROW.*

Where it doth snow red roses,
There it doth rain warm tears!

TO-DAY yet and to-morrow,

My Love, with thee I'll stay,

But when the third day cometh,

I must from here away."

" When wilt return again to

Me, best beloved mine,

And pluck the fairest roses,

And drink the cooling wine?"

" When roses red it snoweth,

And raineth cooling wine;

So long thou'lt have to tarry,

Oh, best beloved mine!"

---

* The author of this peculiar popular song (𝔅𝔢𝔦𝔩𝔰𝔦𝔩𝔢𝔟) was born in the year 1605.

Ging sie in's Vaters Gärtelein,

Legt nieder sich, schlief ein;

Da träumet ihr ein Träumelein,

Wie's regnet kühlen Wein.

Und als sie da erwachte,

Da war es lauter nichts,

Da blühten wohl die Rosen

Und blühten über sie.

Ein Haus thät sie sich bauen

Von lauter grünem Klee,

Thät aus zum Himmel schauen,

Wohl nach dem Rosenschnee.

Into her father's garden

She went, lay down and fell

Asleep, and dreamed 'twas raining

Cool wine by magic spell.

When she awoke, she saw it

Was but an idle dream;

True, roses red were blooming,

And all around did gleam.

She built a house of grasses,

And velvet moss so soft,

And for the snow of roses

Looked up to Heaven oft.

Mit gelb Wachs thät sie's decken,

Mit gelber Lilie rein,

Daß sie sich könnt' verstecken,

Wenn's regnet kühlen Wein.

Und als das Haus gebauet war,

Trank sie den Herrgotts-Wein;

Ein Rosenkränzlein in der Hand,

Schlief sie darinnen ein.

Der Knabe kehrt zürücke,

Geht in den Garten ein,

Trägt einen Kranz von Rosen

Und einen Becher Wein.

With yellow wax she covered

Its roof, and lilies fine,

That she might have a shelter

When it did rain cool wine.

And when it was completed,

God's sacred wine she drank;

And in her hands a rosary,

Calmly in sleep she sank.

The youth returns; behold, to

The garden he hath sped,

Wine in a goblet carries,

And a wreath of roses red.

Hat mit dem Fuß gestoßen

Wohl an das Hügelein,

Er fiel, da schneit' es Rosen,

Da regnet's kühlen Wein.

Simon Dach (Wunderhorn.)

His foot in contact comes with

A little mound—and Oh !

He falls—now cooling wine it

Rains, and roses red dotn snow !

SIMON DACH (WUNDERHORN.)

Spruch.

Wer nicht gelitten, hat nur halb gelebt;

Wer nicht gefehlt, hat wohl auch

nicht geftrebt;

Wer nie geweint, hat halb auch nur gelacht;

Wer nie gezweifelt, hat wohl kaum gedacht!

Julie Burow.

PROVERB.

WHO never knew misfortune, lived
but half;
Who never wept, ne'er heartily did
laugh ;
Who never failed, could scarce have
striv'n and wrought;
Who never doubted, hardly could
have thought.

JULIE BUROW.

Nächtlicher Uebergang der Polen bei Krakau.

Die Lüfte weh'n so schaurig,
    Wir ziehn dahin so traurig

Nach ungewissem Ziel!

Kaum leuchten uns die Sterne;

Europa sieht von Ferne

Das große Trauerspiel.

Uns wendend oft zurücke

Betreten wir die Brücke,

Die uns von Polen trennt.

Bei trübem Fackelbrande

Grüßt uns das Volk am Strande,

Das unsre Leiden kennt.

CROSSING OF THE POLES AT CRACOW UNDER COVER OF NIGHT.*

THE breezes sadly sigh and wail,

 We march along with cheeks so pale,

Impelled by unrelenting Fate.

There lights our way no friendly star

Of hope; Europe sees from afar

The tragedy so mournful, great.

Oft looking back to gaze on friends,

We cross the bridge, our hearts it rends,

That us from glorious Poland parts.

By torchlight dim, they greet our band

And weep, the people on the strand,

Who know the wrongs that break our hearts.

. * This is a paraphrase.

Verkauft, besiegt, verrathen—

Sind unsre besten Thaten,

Wie Träume leer und hohl,

Und lassen keine Spuren;

So nehmt, geliebte Fluren,

Das letzte Lebewohl!

Lebt ewig wohl, o Brüder!

Ein Haufe Lebensmüder

Trifft überall ein Grab.

Nicht uns vom Tod zu retten,

Nein, nur zu fliehn die Ketten,

Ergreifen wir den Stab.

Defeated, sold, and ay, betrayed;

Our noblest deeds, the schemes well layed,

Like idle, empty dreams, dispel,

Leaving behind no single trace.

Farewell then, thou beloved place,

Where we as freemen dwelt, farewell!

Farewell dear brothers, left behind!

Weary of life, we hope to find

A quiet grave in foreign land.

To free ourselves from death and pain?

No, 'twas to flee *dread slavery's* chain,

That made us take the staff in hand!

Wir ziehn von Weib und Kindern,

Vermögen nicht zu hindern

Des Vaterlands Ruin.

Schon lechzt nach unserm Blute

Die Petersburger Knute,

Die Fuchtel von Berlin.

Ein thränenloses Wesen

Ward uns zum Herrn erlesen,

Versteint und ungebeugt.

Aus möderischem Stamme

Trägt seine Stirn die Schramme,

Die sein Geschlecht bezeugt.

From children, wife and friends we part,

Our country's waste with throbbing heart

We see, yet cannot stay the flood.

The dreadful knout of barbarous Russia,

The whip laid on by heartless Prussia,

Cry loud for blood, for Polish blood.

A wretch, a cold and tearless thing,

Was forced upon us as our king,

With heart of stone, to horrors weaned,

Descended from a murd'rous line,

He on his forehead bears the sign

That tells mankind—he is a fiend.

Die wir jedoch erwarben,

Deck' uns, o Ruhm, die Narben,

Mach' unsre Namen klar.

Du machst den Schmerz gesetzter,

Denn unsres Volkes Letzter

Ist größer als der Czar.

Uns bleibt nur ein Vermächtniß:

Des edlen Kampfs Gedächtniß,

Der Polen neu verband,

Des langen Kriegs Beschwerde

Und eine Hand voll Erde

Aus unserm Vaterland.

Thou whom we justly won, Oh, Fame,

To all the world display our name,

And cover thou the bleeding scar.

Then all our wounds do cease to ache,

For from our midst the humblest take,

And he is greater than the Czar.

We have one gift for all that's done :

The thought of battles fought and won,

That were to forge our National band ;

The memory of our bloody toil,

And a hand full of that sacred soil

From Poland dear, our fatherland.

O selig jene, welche

Berauscht vom Todeskelche,

Gesunken sind im Streit,

Und ihr, Volhyniens Söhne,

Die aus dem Angstgestöhne

Die feuchte Gruft befreit!

Sie drangen auf den Rossen,

Von Feinden fest umschlossen,

Zum Weichselufer vor,

An fremden Strand zu schiffen;

Da schwoll von Schmerz ergriffen

Ihr groß Gemüth empor.

Oh! fortunate and happy they,

On whom his fingers Death did lay,

Whilst fighting hard for liberty.

And ye, Volhynia's sons so brave,

Whom from this moment's trial, the grave

So damp and cool, set quickly free!

Surrounded by their bitter foe,

They pressed ahead with silent woe

To the Vistula's banks, there to embark,

To leave their home forevermore;

Then swelled their hearts, with anguish
   sore,
And to the promptings all did hark.

Sie konnten's nicht ertragen,

Der Heimath abzusagen,

Die jeden Wunsch umschloß

Da stürzten sich die Guten

Hinunter in die Fluthen

Mit Waffen und mit Roß.

O vaterländ'sche Wellen,

Die längst vom Blute schwellen,

Nehmt euch der Todten an!

Ihr dürft das Meer erreichen,

So wälzt die freien Leichen

Zum freien Ozean!

August Graf von Platen.

They wavered, for they could not bear

Themselves from home, sweet home to
    tear,

Where centered then their every thought.

And so with arms and horse they throw

Themselves into the stream below,—

Since lost the cause for which they fought.

Receive then, Oh! ye friendly waves,

Though red with blood, these martyred
    braves,

And float them on from place to place,

Till, when ye reach the open sea,

Ye may the corpses of the free

Give to the Ocean's free embrace.

AUGUST COUNT VON PLATEN.

Spruch.

Die Freundschaft währt ewig,
    Die Liebe vergeht:
D'rum wähle die Freundschaft,
Die ewig besteht.

Die Liebe bringt Rosen,
Die Freundschaft bringt Ruh',
D'rum wähle sie beide;—
Wie glücklich bist du!

Ungenannt.

PROVERB.

FRIENDSHIP is lasting,
　　Love passeth away.
Therefore choose friendship,
That ever doth stay.

Love bringeth roses,
Friendship brings rest,
Both having chosen,
Indeed thou art blest.

ANONYMOUS.

Meiner Mutter.

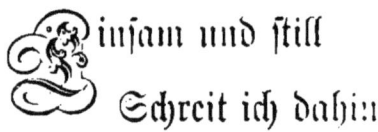insam und still
Schreit ich dahin
Im fremden Land.

Die Heimath fern,

Die traute Heimath,

Die Jugend vorbei,

Die glückselige Jugend,

Und mein Liebstes, mein Theuerstes

Nun im Grab,

Auch du—o Mutter!

Still ist dein Herz,

Das so lange geschlagen

Für mich allein

In Leid und Lust,

TO MY MOTHER.

ONELY and still
  I roam about
In foreign lands.

Sweet home far away,

My beloved home,

The bright days of my youth

Forevermore gone,

And my dearest, best loved, all

In the grave.

Thou too, Oh, mother!

Still is thy heart

That so long did beat fondly

For me alone,

In grief and joy,—

Das treue, das heilige
Mutterherz.—
Geschlossen dein Aug',
Das so manche Stunde
Gewacht und geweint
Um mich allein.

Und es modert die Hand,
Die liebe Hand,
Die so oft mich gestreichelt
In seliger Zeit;
Herz, Aug' und Hand
Und all' deine Liebe,
Hast Alles genommen
Mit hinein
In's dunkle, in's schaurige
Grab—o Mutter!

The true, the holy

Motherheart.

Closed is thy eye,

That many an hour

Did watch and weep

For me alone.

And thy hand is mouldering,

The lovely hand,

That so often caressed me

In happy days.

Heart, eyes and *hand,*

And all thy *love*

Hast taken with thee

Down into

The dark and fearful

Grave,—Oh, mother!

Und es fällt mein Blick

Auf das weiße Linnen,

Das kühl und lind

Den Leib mir umhüllt.

Aus Heimathserde

Grünte hervor,

Dicht hinter des Gartens

Süßduftender Hecke

Wuchs und blühte

Der blaue Lein;

Im Elternhause

Ward er bereitet

Und schimmerte hell

Und seidenweich

Als buschiger Rocken.

Im Wohngemach,

And my gaze doth fall

Upon the white linen

That cool and soft

Encircles my body.

On that field at home,

So green and fresh,

Close back of the garden's

Sweet fragrant copse,

Did bloom and grow

The flax so blue;

In my parents' house

It was prepared :

It glimmered so bright,

So silky, and fine,

On the bushy rock.

In the cozy apartment,

Bei traulicher Lampe

Saßest und spannst du,

Indeß ich dir vorlaß

Aus Deutschlands Dichtern;

Und jeder Faden,

Durch deine Finger

Ist er geglitten,

Die lieben Finger

Haben geweiht ihn,

Die oft mir die glühende

Wange gestreichelt

Und selig geruht

Auf des fröhlichen Knaben

Blondem Gelock.

Und tausend Wünsche,

Fromme, heilige

By the lamp's mild reflection,

I can see thee sitting

And quietly spinning,

While I read aloud

From Germany's Poets ;

And every thread did

Glide through thy fingers,

Thou fondest of mothers !

And was consecrated

By those lovely fingers,

That softly caressed

So often my cheeks,

And happy did rest

On the flaxen ringlets

Of the merry boy.

And thousand wishes,

Segenswünsche
Spannst du mit hinein,
Mutter—Mutter.—
Ich fühle, ich fühl' es,
Aus des Gewebes
Verschlungenen Fäden
Strömet dein Segen
Mir in's vereinsamte
Trauernde Herz.—
Und trostvoll heimisch
Wird mir zu Muth,
Als ob du selbst
Mit den theuren Armen
Liebend und schützend
Still mich umfingst,
Mutter,—Mutter!

Hermann Allmers.

Sacred and holy,

Wishes of blessing,

Didst spin in with it,

Mother,—mother!

I feel it, I feel it,

Out of the texture's

Fine woven threads

Floweth thy blessing

Into my lonely heart;

And I feel a consoling

And home-like influence,

As if thou, Oh, mother!

Protecting and loving,

With thy dearest arms, didst

Silently embrace me,—

Mother,—mother!

HERMANN ALLMERS.

Mein und Dein.

Das Mägdlein sprach: „Lieb Knabe
mein,

Nun sag' mir, was ist mein und dein?"

Der Knabe sprach: „Lieb Mädchen mein,

Dein schönes Auge das ist dein,

Und drein zu schauen, das ist mein;

Dein rother süßer Mund ist dein,

Dich drauf zu küssen, das ist mein;

Nun thu' mir auf die Arme dein,

Drin liegen das ist dein und mein."

Johann G. Fischer.

MINE AND THINE.

THE maiden said: " Beloved mine,

Do tell me, what is mine and thine?"

The youth replied: "Sweet maiden mine,

Thy lovely eye, though that is thine,

Therein to gaze, ah, that is mine;

Thy mouth so red and sweet is thine,

Thereon to kiss thee, that is mine;

Now open wide those arms of thine,

Therein to lie, is thine and mine."

JOHANN G. FISCHER.

Das Erkennen.

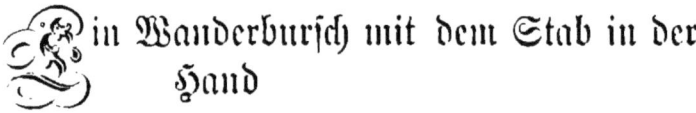in Wanderbursch mit dem Stab in der
Hand

Kommt wieder heim aus dem fremden Land.

Sein Haar ist bestäubt, sein Antlitz verbrannt;

Von wem wird der Bursch wohl zuerst er-
kannt?

So tritt er in's Städtchen, in's alte Thor,

Am Schlagbaum lehnt just der Zöllner davor.

Doch sieh'—Freund Zollmann erkennt ihn
nicht,

Zu sehr hat die Sonn' ihm verbrannt das
Gesicht.

Und weiter wandert nach kurzem Gruß

Der Bursch und schüttelt den Staub von dem
Fuß.

Da schaut aus dem Fenster sein Schätzlein
fromm:

„Du blühende Jungfrau, viel schönen Will-
komm!"

THE RECOGNITION.

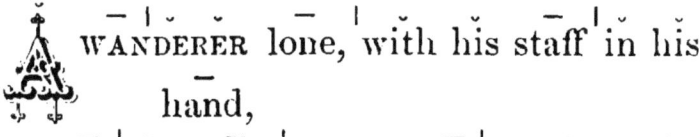

A WANDERER lone, with his staff in his
    hand,
Returneth home from a far distant land.

He is covered with dust and bronzed is
    his face,
Who will first give him a welcome embrace?

He enters the town through the ancient
    gate,
Where the toller leans out at the window
    grate,
But there's no welcome smile in friend
    tollman's gaze :
Too much the youth's bronzed by the
    sun's burning rays.
With a hasty nod he the toller doth greet,

And passing on, stamps the dust from his
    feet.
Lo, from yon window his maiden doth
    stare—
He calleth, "God greet thee, maiden fair!"

Doch sieh'—auch das Mädchen erkennt ihn
nicht,

Die Sonn' hat zu sehr ihm verbrannt das
Gesicht.

Und weiter geht er die Straße entlang,

Ein Thränlein hängt ihm an der braunen
Wang'.

Da wankt von dem Kirchstieg das Mütterlein
her;

„Gott grüß' Euch!" so spricht er, und sonst
Nichts mehr.

Doch sieh'—das Mütterlein schluchzet vor Lust:

„Mein Sohn!" und sinkt an des Burschen
Brust.

Wie sehr auch die Sonne sein Antlitz ver=
brannt,

Das Mutterang' hat ihn doch gleich erkannt.

Johann N. Vogl.

But even his Love doth vacantly gaze:

Too much he is bronzed by the sun's burning rays.

And farther he walks, now so sad and meek,

A tear trickling down his sunburnt cheek.

Now his mother totters from yon church door;

"God greet thee!" he speaketh, and nothing more,

But look, the mother is sobbing for joy:

"My son!" and falls on the breast of her boy.

Though the sun did bronze him so as to disguise —

His mother did him at once recognize.

JOHANN N. VOGL.

Des Waldes Kind.

In Waldes Nacht bin ich geboren,
    In Waldes Dunkel stand mein Haus,
Da lebt' ich einsam, wie verloren,
Und sehnte nimmer mich heraus.

Der erste Ton, der mir erklungen,
War Waldes Flüstern leis' und lind;
Der Wald hat mir ein Lied gesungen,
Wie eine Mutter ihrem Kind.

Und diesem Ton, so langsam leise,
Ihm lauschte ernst des Kindes Ohr,
Schon klang ihm aus der düst'ren Weise
Der süße Inhalt traulich vor

THE FOREST CHILD.

IN forest night there was I born,
  In woodland darkness stood my cot,
I lived recluse, as if forlorn,
Yet never craved a different lot.

The sound that first my heart did thrill
Crept through the foliage soft and mild;
The forest sang an air so still,
E'en like a mother to her child.

I heard the song so strange and new,
A cradled child with wonder rude,
Till all its sweetest meanings grew
From out the darkness of its mood.

Als ich gesetzt aus meinem Hause
Zum ersten Mal den jungen Fuß,
Erklang durch Flüstern und Gebrause
Für mich des Waldes trauter Gruß.

Und ich vestand des Waldes Worte,
Er sprach: sei mir gegrüßt, mein Kind!
Gegrüßt am heilig stummen Orte!
So klang's zu mir im Abendwind.

Und weiter sprach er: jedem Kinde
Ziemt ein Geschenk von Vaters Hand,
So wähle, was zum Angebinde
Dein junges Herz am schönsten fand.

And when at last from home I stirred,

A happy child, the world to see,

Go where I would, I ever heard

The welcome song of the forest tree.

The forest's words I understood:

" Innocent child, thou'rt welcome here;

Welcome unto this holy wood,

In evening calm, in morning clear!"

And more it said: " As every child

Longs for a gift from father hand,

So choose ought in this woodland wild

To take with thee from land to land!"

Ich aber sprach: so lehr' mich singen
Wie das, was rauschend dich durchweht
Von dem die Berge mächtig klingen,
Was sanft vom Baum zu Baume geht.

Was süß aus jedem Vogel schallend
So stark ergreift die Menschenbrust,
Und was die Quelle, weiter wallend,
Erzählt, sich selber unbewußt.

So sprach ich, und in alter Weise
Des Waldes Wipfel rauschten lind,
Und es ertönte flüsternd leise:
Dir sei's gewährt, mein liebes Kind!

Reinhold Mund.

I answered thus : "Teach me to sing

Like that which gently breathes through
    thee,
When all the hills are murmuring,

And music swells from tree to tree ;

Which from the wildbird in the sun,

Thrills with the sweet content it gives,

And the streamlet, as it floweth on,

Relates, unconscious that it lives."

Thus I did speak,—as it chances oft,

The old tree tops then rustled mild,

Wafting to me a whisper soft :

"'Tis granted thee, thou lovely child!"

REINHOLD MUND.

Wenn du noch eine Heimath hast.

Wenn du noch eine Heimath hast,-
So nimm den Ranzen und den Stecken,
Und wand're, wand're ohne Rast,
Bis du erreicht den theuren Flecken.

Und strecken nur zwei Arme sich
In freud'ger Sehnsucht dir entgegen,
Fließt eine Thräne nur um dich,
Spricht dir ein einz'ger Mund den Segen,

Ob du ein Bettler, du bist reich,
Ob krank dein Herz, dein Muth beklommen,
Gesunden wirst du allsogleich,
Hörst du das süße Wort : Willkommen !

IF THOU DOST STILL POSSESS A HOME.

IF thou dost still possess a home,

Take up thy staff, Oh, linger not,

And roam, care not for rest, but roam,

Till thou hast reached the treasured spot.

If but two arms extended be

To thee in friendly longing near,

Oh! doth one tear but flow for thee,

A blessing speak one mouth sincere :

Wert thou a beggar, thou hadst wealth.

Wert sick at heart, thy spirit wound :

At once thou wilt regain thy health,

Hear'st, "Welcome home" that sweetest
    sound.

Und ist verweht auch jede Spur,

Zeigt nichts sich deinem Blick, dem nassen,

Als grün berast ein Hügel nur

Von Allem, was du einst verlassen:

O, nirgend weint es sich so gut,

Wie weit dich deine Füße tragen,

Als da, wo still ein Herze ruht,

Das einstens warm für dich geschlagen.

Albert Traeger.

Although no traces may be found,

Nothing may meet thy swimming eye,

But green o'er-run a little mound,

Of all thou once didst bid, "good bye ; "

Oh ! nowhere canst thou weep so well,

Wherever carry thee thy feet,

As where in death a heart doth dwell,

That once for thee did warmly beat.

ALBERT TRÆGER.

Der Rehſchädel.

Einſam lag ich im Walde
    Im tiefen Schatten da,
Als eines Rehes Schädel
Im Moos ich liegen ſah.

Das zarteſte Gehörne
Stieg bleich und weiß empor;
Der Epheu hielt's umſponnen,
Wuchs überall hervor.

Es brachen große Blumen
Aus dieſem kleinen Haus,
Und aus den Augenhöhlen
Sah'n freundlich ſie heraus.

THE DEER-SKULL.

WHILE lying in the forest,
  In shade and solitude,
I in the moss beside me
A curious deer-skull viewed.

So pale and white its antlers
Rose up before my view,
Around them twined the ivy,
Forth everywhere it grew.

Out of this little dwelling
Large flowers did thickly creep,
From out the eyeless sockets
So friendly they did peep.

So schienen aus dem Schädel

Zwei blaue Augen klar;

Nicht wußt' ich, ob er lebend,

Ob wirklich todt er war.

Ich sprach: wird Todt zum Leben,

Das Leben so zum Tod?

Seid ihr so eng verschwistert,

Was hat es dann für Noth!

Ob nun, wann ich gestorben,

Im hellen Jugendgrün

Auf meinem Todtenschädel

Noch meine Lieder blüh'n?

Julius Mosen.

Thus from the skull, a pair of

Blue eyes their lustre shed;

I knew not if 'twas living,

Or if 'twas really dead.

I spoke : turns Death to Life thus,

And Life to Death ? so near

If ye are both related—

Why need we have a fear ?

Have I from life departed

In early Spring, Oh! will

Upon my skull, I wonder,

My Songs bloom brightly still ?

JULIUS MOSEN.

Verzeichniss der Dichter.

(364)

LIST OF AUTHORS

(365)